31/5

the
smoke-free
smoke break

Stop Smoking Now with Mindfulness & Acceptance

Pavel G. Somov, PhD
Marla J. Somova, PhD

New Harbinger Publications, Inc.

Publisher's Note

Distributed in Canada by Raincoast Books

Copyright © 2011 by Pavel G. Somov and Marla J. Somova
New Harbinger Publications, Inc.
5674 Shattuck Avenue
Oakland, CA 94609
www.newharbinger.com

Cover design by Amy Shoup; Text design by Michele Waters-Kermes; Acquired by Melissa Kirk; Edited by Nelda Street

All Rights Reserved

Printed in the United States of America

Library of Congress Cataloging in Publication Data

Somov, Pavel G.
 The smoke-free smoke break : stop smoking now with mindfulness and acceptance / Pavel G. Somov and Marla J. Somova ; foreword by Andrew Tatarsky.
   p. cm.
 Includes bibliographical references.
 ISBN 978-1-60882-001-6 (pbk.) -- ISBN 978-1-60882-002-3 (pdf e-book)
 1. Smoking cessation. 2. Mindfulness-based cognitive therapy. 3. Smoking--Psychological aspects. I. Somova, Marla J. II. Title.
 HV5740.S65 2011
 616.86'506--dc23

                         2011027864

13   12   11
10   9   8   7   6   5   4   3   2   1
First printing

Contents

Part 4 Landing Gear: Recovery-Maintenance Skills

Part 5 The Final Approach: Testing and Quitting

Part 6 Destination Harm Reduction: Mindful Smoking

Foreword

Welcome to Pavel Somov and Marla Somova's guide to changing your
relationship to smoking, whether that means quitting, cutting back, or
simply smoking more mindfully. This groundbreaking book is both a state-
of-the-art, research-supported, practical manual for breaking the habit
and a compassionate guide to waking up and becoming fully present in
your life. I am deeply grateful for the gift of this book, and I am certain
that you will feel the same as you work and play your way through it.

From the first page, I was riveted. Having worked professionally with
addictive behavior for thirty years, I am seldom surprised by new ideas. Yet
this book surprised me with many delightful, inspiring, and useful ideas
and exercises that I immediately began to bring into my work with patients.

This book rides the crest of a new, hopeful, and effective approach to
positive behavior change that's revolutionizing the way professionals
understand and address addictive behaviors. We are emerging from a dark,
pessimistic age in which addictive behaviors, such as smoking, were viewed
as permanent, chronic diseases that only complete and total abstinence
could heal. Therein, "addicts" were stigmatized as powerless and controlled by their disease. The prognosis was poor because these people were
seen as merely responding to negative social sanctions and requiring coer-
cive treatments that, unfortunately, failed the overwhelming majority.
This failure was attributed to the disease and the "addict's" lack of motivation—a bleak picture indeed!

While this scenario is more frequently associated with the "harder"
addictions, it is also applied in more subtle ways to the smoking "addict,"
reflected in the current embrace of increasingly punitive, unsympathetic

social attitudes and actions toward smokers, such as increasing taxes on cigarettes to an extent way out of proportion with other recreational activities. I and others have critiqued the biologically reductionistic view that blames the evil drug or the "addict's" moral weakness while missing the complexity of the smoker's relationship to smoking. Inadequate understanding of the behavior and the resulting inadequate treatments explain the poor outcomes of treatment and self-help approaches. This book explores this stigmatization of smokers in greater depth and discusses why smokers warrant compassion, acceptance, and respect, which are essential for developing a healthier relationship to smoking.

The emerging paradigm offers a more complex and positive understanding of why people develop addictive behaviors, and it suggests more effective approaches to changing them. This increasingly accepted approach understands addictive behaviors as being related to a complex interplay of biology, psychology, and social context that is unique for each person. Addictive behaviors reflect a variety of positive, adaptive motives that need to be recognized and appreciated before work on behavior change can be successful, motives that include the need to cope with stress and other difficult feelings and life circumstances, to care for oneself, and to seek pleasure and enjoyment and the related social experiences. Addictive behaviors always have positive aspects that attract people to them. People smoke and use other substances because it feels good and works in some vital ways, even when the behavior may have serious short- and long-term associated risks. This view sees smokers and other drug users as people who are responsible for their choices, and it approaches the question of why people make these choices with compassion, empathy, and respect. This adaptive viewpoint explains why people begin smoking and find it pleasurable, and it also provides a way to consider what issues may need to be addressed to support a choice to stop or reduce smoking. Our understanding of behavioral conditioning provides a model for understanding how, ever so subtly over time, the initial choice to smoke can become a deeply ingrained, irresistible overlearned habit that is very difficult to change—in the authors' words, from mindful choice to mindless habit. This understanding of addictive behaviors suggests that an effective approach to changing them requires both recognizing the positive functions of the behavior and employing a strategic approach to change these deeply ingrained habits. This book offers the solution: meet the mindlessness of habit with a mindful awareness that enables the smoker to confront powerful urges with an alternative solution or response that reinforces a new pathway.

This book beautifully brings these ideas to life in a way that is clear, compelling, and inspiring. The authors teach a comprehensive mindfulness-based craving-control technique for "awakening the smoking zombie" and turning mindless habitual smoking into mindful smoking, a process that literally extinguishes the smoking habit. Not only will you learn how to break the habit step by step, but—and this is the real payoff—you will also be introduced to mindfulness practice in the process! The authors will show you how to actually use your smoking urges as reminders to meditate and cultivate a greater capacity to be more fully present to yourself and your life. Their technique brings together mindfulness practice and relaxing breathing through many creative exercises and provocative koans designed to teach and provoke, encourage and seduce awakening. Like wise old Zen teachers, the authors are sometimes gentle and loving, and sometimes funny and perplexing, and they always invite deep introspection, recasting the hard work of quitting smoking as an exciting adventure of self-discovery.

This book places importance on your really learning the skills and craving-control strategies and demonstrating your ability to use them before attempting to quit. The authors suggest that premature attempts to quit or stay quit with inadequate preparation are usually what sets smokers up for failure, but the approach they teach will prepare you well for your chosen quit date. In fact, you are encouraged to continue smoking as a necessary part of the process of learning the skills you need to quit. You will smoke your way to quitting and won't be asked to quit until you are ready!

Harm-reduction principles, which make up my personal and professional philosophy for living, deeply inform this book. Called "compassionate pragmatism" by trailblazing addictive behavior researcher Alan Marlatt, harm reduction asserts that all effective strategies must really start where people are, with their unique, complex subjective experience. There must be pragmatic acceptance that people are where they are, as well as compassion for any struggles and suffering linked to the problem behavior. Harm reduction recognizes all positive change as success, even if it's just steps in a positive direction rather than stopping altogether. We don't need to know the end point of the journey toward healing, growth, and positive change in order to begin the journey. Although it's great if you commit to quitting smoking, you aren't required to before starting the process of cutting down. You will feel welcome here whether you are simply concerned about your smoking and want to examine it more fully, are considering cutting back, or are clear that you want to stop.

As if all of this were not enough, the authors end the book with useful discussions about caring for yourself once you have quit or cut back, offering many strategies to reduce and prevent relapse. The ideas and strategies that this book brings together are all evidence supported, the new standard for good treatment and self-help strategies. This book will be useful both to people working on their smoking and to professionals seeking tools to add to their support toolboxes.

With wisdom, wit, creativity, and humor, the authors take you on a journey that begins with support for addressing your smoking, then expands to encompass ways that you can attain better health and greater awareness and enjoyment of life. I wish you a wonderful, enlightening journey.

—Andrew Tatarsky, PhD
　　Center for Integrative Harm Reduction Psychotherapy,
　　New York

Introduction

Over thirty-five years ago, in *Stop without Quitting*, Joseph Danysh (1974, 2–3) provided this wise caution against impulse-driven attempts to quit smoking: "[I]f you are a smoker, while you're reading this book, you should continue to light up whenever you feel like it. There are no tricks involved in this, only a delayed fuse that works its own magical way.... Patience, curiosity, and a certain tolerance for ideas are your best allies for now." The smoking cessation industry, of course, didn't listen. Like all addiction industries, "big smoking cessation" (just like "big tobacco") doesn't mind a revolving door; after all, relapse is just repeat business. So, here we are, still trying to scare people with warnings from the surgeon general, rushing smokers into premature abstinence on nothing but a patch and a prayer.

When we sat down to document our clinical experience with smoking cessation, we didn't know about Danysh's flash-in-the-pan attempt to revamp smoking-cessation treatment in the 1970s. What we did know was that contemporary smoking-cessation self-help approaches barely work. Relapse rates are as high as 98 percent (Garvey et al. 1992) and parallel those of heroin users (Hunt and Bespalec 1974). Of these smoking-cessation efforts, 75 percent take a nosedive within the very first week, over 40 percent fail within the first fourteen days, and 95 percent are history within a year (West and Shiffman 2007; Garvey et al. 1992). So, hold your unbridled enthusiasm, smoker, and roll up your sleeves to do some "quit-prep work," some experientially fun, thought-provoking, awareness-building, epiphany-instilling, habit-modifying, mindfulness-powered work. And, of course, keep on smoking for now.

Opening *any* book is a commitment of time and mind. Opening a book like this, a self-help book on how to quit smoking, would seem to require an even greater kind of commitment, a commitment to quit using tobacco. But that's not the case, at least, not the way we see it. This book, just like smoking itself, is no one thing. What it actually is depends on who is reading it.

This book is, first and foremost, for those who want to quit smoking. The program we lay out in this book is a total break from the familiar smoking-cessation fare, a paradigm shift (we hope) that some will likely see as near blasphemy. What we offer is no-nonsense boot-camp–length "skillpower" training. So, leave your willpower at the door; you won't need it. In the words of Joseph Danysh (1974, 101), we are going to mount a "flank attack."

If, for the time being, you just want to cut back (which is entirely rational since tobacco-related health problems are dosage dependent), then we have seven *harm-reduction* paths that will take you from *quantity*-based, mindless chain-smoking to *quality*-focused, mindful smoking.

Quitting smoking can bring weight gain for both men and women. Women who quit, for example, gain an average of eight pounds in the first six months to one year (Hudmon et al. 1999). So, if you are a smoker with weight-management concerns, then this book is a "twofer": we offer you systematic, mindfulness-based craving-control training that will enable you to quit smoking as well as manage any mindless, compensatory short-term overeating that may ensue after you quit and potentially undermine your recovery in the long term.

From a Smoking Habit to a Self-Awareness Habit

The craving-control method that we offer in this program is a mindfulness-meditation approach that has been customized for smoking-cessation needs. Quitting a habit like smoking offers you a unique opportunity for meditation. Long after you quit, for days, months, and possibly even years, you will experience recurrent, if only occasional, cravings to light up. You don't have to experience these moments as struggle or strife; you can view them as potential moments to experience enlightening self-awareness. So, as you look ahead, rather than dread the task of quitting or the subsequent cravings, allow yourself to appreciate that quitting this habit comes with the benefit of built-in wake-up calls to meditation. Recognize that it is precisely because you have such a strong habit of smoking that you are uniquely positioned to cultivate a habit of self-awareness. For example, if you were not a smoker and decided today to begin a serious meditation practice, then each and every day, you would have to make a conscious choice to remember to set aside time to meditate. As a smoker who is about to quit, you don't have to busy yourself with any of this: each craving you experience will remind you of the opportunity for meditation. And, since much of your smoking is a form of stress management and coping, chances are that the cravings you will experience will be perfectly timed; in other words, you will develop cravings to smoke exactly at a time when you would benefit the most from a meditation break. Recognize this amazing opportunity and celebrate this unexpected potential benefit of quitting. So, whether your goal is to quit or just cut back, we hope that this book will serve as a meditation mirror to help you glimpse that sense of self that is just as ephemeral as the cigarette smoke itself.

Part 1

Flying High: The Psychology of Smoking and Quitting

Each habit is on its own behavioral orbit, with its own pull and gravity and with its own vicious circle of stop-and-go attempts at quitting. In this part of the book, we will run a few laps around the habit of smoking to get a nonjudgmental, 360-degree view of smoking psychology as such. In addition to exploring the habit of smoking, we will also focus on the perils of another related habit, that of impulsive, premature, drive-through attempts at quitting. Our goal in this book is to not only help you quit smoking but also help you quit quitting.

Chapter 1

Smoking as Such

Are there many other ways—as simple as lighting a
cigarette—to obtain at will... either such a useful
stimulating effect which helps us work at night for a number
of hours, or a reassuring distance between us and the
problem... , as a sedative drug would do?

—Pierre Creyssel,
Electrophysiological Effects of Nicotine

If you are a smoker, chances are that you are in love with smoking. Talking anyone out of love is a fool's business. You know how it is: you fall in love with the "wrong" person, and every significant and not-so-significant other tries to tell you that so-and-so is toxic for you, that this person just isn't a healthy long-term match for you. And, both intellectually and deep inside, you know it's true, but frankly, it just doesn't matter. Then some time goes by, perhaps you catch a glimpse of someone new, and poof! Old love is over, and new love is afoot. What we have set out to do with this book is introduce you to that new someone. Specifically, we'd like to see if you can fall in love with unfiltered breathing, or, as we call it, *smoking air*.

A 360-Degree View of Smoking

Reality isn't just some objective thing that everyone sees the same way. It is an interplay of what objectively "is" and how we subjectively perceive it. Put differently, what you see is what you choose to see. There's far more to smoking than meets the eye. Here's our view of the psychology of smoking.

Smoking Is Behavior

In its most basic sense, smoking is a behavior. Indeed, smoking isn't a thing or a person but a thing that a person does—that is, a behavior.

Smoking Is a Habitual Behavior

Smoking is a high-frequency, repetitive behavior—that is, a habit. Some things, like getting married, people do only once or only once in a while. Smoking is the sort of thing most smokers do a lot. Some smokers chain-smoke a few packs a day, pretty much nonstop. Others might pace themselves through half a pack a day. While smoking rates vary, most active smokers engage in enough smoking behavior on a daily basis for smoking to become habitual. Any behavior that is repeated enough times tends to start running on autopilot, becoming mindless and "second nature."

Smoking Is Chemical Coping

Nicotine is a paradoxical drug. Smoking both excites and calms. This habit has been shown to improve performance, reaction time, and information processing, while simultaneously stabilizing a person's emotional tone, which is apparently due to "a periodic pattern of arousal and alertness during smoking, followed by calming and tension reduction after smoking" (Antonuccio and Boutilier 2000, 238).

What this means is that smokers smoke to regulate how they feel—that is, to cope. Coping comes in two broad flavors (and, no, we're not talking "regular" and "menthol"). You can cope internally (through breathing, meditation, self-talk), or you can outsource coping using chemicals. When you drink alcohol or take prescription psychiatric medications (although some people certainly need the latter), you are coping through chemistry. It's the same with smoking: it's nothing other than chemically assisted emotional *self-regulation*—that is, a way to use chemicals to feel better, less stressed, more energetic, and so on.

Smoking as a Rational Pursuit of Well-Being

As a form of coping, smoking is the pursuit of well-being. Any coping is. The point of coping is to feel better. Thus, smoking is a form of self-help—that is, a form of self-care. As such, smoking is entirely rational. Any notion that smoking is self-destructive or irrational is an utter misunderstanding of the psychology of smoking. Case in point: it's Monday; you feel stressed out, so you step out for a smoke break, for a "breather" of sorts, to get away from whatever it is that's bumming you out, so you can relax and feel better. On some level you know it's not good for your body in the long run. True, but that doesn't negate the fact that your motive to smoke is to help yourself feel better *now*. And now is where it's at. "Now" isn't just a word; it's your entire life. The authors of *The Smoking Puzzle: Information, Risk Perception, and Choice* write (Sloan, Smith, and Taylor 2003, 25): "For some, cigarettes provide a 'comfort,' a 'friend' in times of stress, and a benefit that outweighs all other consequences." The bottom line is that the motivation behind smoking is self-care, and there's nothing irrational about trying to cope.

Smoking as a Tactical Gain with a Strategic Cost

Tactical (short-term) behavior aims to change something immediately, whereas *strategic* (long-term) behavior, by definition, takes a longer view of change. For example, going to the movies tonight will help you feel better *tonight*, in the shorter term. Enrolling in college today will help you get a better job in the distant future, years from now, in the longer term. Get this: *all coping is tactical behavior*. All coping is designed to reduce your immediate distress. All coping is motivated by the prospect of short-term gains. But, of course, not all coping is created equal. Some self-help coping behavior, such as smoking, comes at great strategic cost. Indeed, you feel bummed out, so you decide to solve this problem by lighting up. The cost of this coping solution is the price of the cigarette and seven minutes off your life expectancy (Mackay, Eriksen, and Shafey 2006). Is this too great of a strategic cost? Can you afford this kind of solution? The answer depends entirely on your priorities and the psychological resources at hand. If it takes a cigarette to keep you off the ledge, then wasting seven minutes of your life expectancy may save you years. Cope with what you've got until you've had a chance to systematically upgrade your coping software.

Smoking as an Expression of Mind-over-Body Values

As a smoker, you probably haven't thought of yourself as a health nut, but in a way, you are. Let us explain. One way of looking at ourselves is to say that we are a combination of body and mind. Both are equally important halves of one human whole, right? In theory, yes. In practice, no. People differ in terms of what they value more. Some value physical health more than mental health. Others place mental health over physical health. Both sets of priorities are existentially valid. Indeed, who is arrogant enough to definitively proclaim that you'd do better with an unhealthy mind in a healthy body than with a healthy mind in an unhealthy body? It's a classic existential dilemma, and whatever you decide is okay by us. We are clinical libertarians who feel that it's simply nobody's business to tell you what you should value more in your life, your body or your mind.

Thus, as a form of coping, smoking is an expression of mind-over-body values. Indeed, when you choose to cope (which is mind business), you are paying for your emotional well-being with your body as the coin. In other words, just like your classic body-focused health nut who gets up at dawn to run a 5K or drive to a yoga session, you, too, are going to extremes to maintain your health—the health of your mind, that is.

As such, smoking is a *coping extreme* in which the mind's short-term well-being is obtained at potentially grave long-term risks to the body. But guess what? This kind of extreme coping at the expense of the body is common. Take extreme sports, for example. People risk bodily health and even life itself just to get a mental kick by climbing cliffs and jumping out of planes. Whether you join the military, become a cop, or go on a humanitarian-relief mission in a war zone, you are essentially chasing mental health, a fix of existential meaning at potentially life-threatening costs. After all, pride, honor, and a sense of accomplishment are all just forms of mental well-being. And, as a society, we generally see nothing wrong with paying dearly for this kind of psychological health with the voucher of the body. So coping by smoking is nothing other than a choice of psychological self-care at the expense of the body. Are there other ways of coping? Of course. But that's not the point—at least not yet. The point is that as a smoker who is paying for emotional well-being with the body, there is no need for you to second-guess your sanity. You are doing what all of us are doing, in one form or another. The only issue is that you are overpaying: buying a moment of emotional well-being at too great of an expense to your body.

Smoking as Consciousness Modifier

People smoke tobacco because nicotine is a psychoactive drug. *Psychoactive* drugs activate your psyche—that is, alter your mind. That's "better living through chemistry," and as we see it, there is fundamentally nothing wrong with that. After all, people do it all the time when they drink coffee, eat chocolate, or take a pill to reduce anxiety or alleviate depression. Smoking, as a coping behavior, works because it changes your state of mind. And that's the whole point of coping. All coping is designed to alter the mind, to reactivate the psyche in the direction of pleasure, significance, and well-being. In other words, all coping is psychoactive, mind altering, and consciousness modifying by design—even the kind of coping that involves inhaling nothing more than *unfiltered* air. Speaking of which…

Smoking as Breath-Focused Coping

Smoking, as we see it, isn't just about inhalation of tobacco. It's also about the process of inhalation and exhalation itself. Indeed, smoking is indistinguishable from your run-of-the-mill deep-breathing exercise, except that you are inhaling junk air rather than unfiltered Mother-Nature air. Did you know that much of what makes deep breathing relaxing is the prolonged exhalation phase of breathing? For breathing relaxation to be most effective, it helps to slow down your breathing rate to extend the amount of time that it takes for you to expel the air from your lungs— which is pretty much what happens when you smoke: you inhale, you hold, and then you slowly exhale. And voilà: you feel relaxed. Our guess is that much of what you enjoy about smoking isn't tobacco itself, but the relaxing subtleties of the slow-smoking behavior—that is, the inherent relaxation of the breath work itself.

Smoking as a Platform for Meditation

Edward Bulwer-Lytton (quoted in Kuntz 1997, 82) once said, "The [person] who smokes thinks like a sage." Exactly, for there is more to smoking than meets the eye. What you have, in fact, developed is an excellent platform of breath-focused, contemplative coping. Indeed, like a devoted monk, for years, you have been breaking away from the rat race or the daily grind into brief and effective meditative retreats. While you have been certainly poisoning yourself with the junk tobacco air, at the same time, you have taken time to cope. Indeed, you have developed what we see as an invaluable habit: "dosing" yourself with "paced" contemplative, breath-focused self-care.

Nonsmokers aren't generally so attuned to their coping needs. They mostly plow through the day, and if they are conscientious about psychological self-care, they might sit down to meditate at some point. You, however, have chosen a different path, a path that makes a lot of sense: you've been coping on demand. You have mastered an important existential skill, that of putting life on hold and taking the exit ramp for a few minutes of coping solitude, reassuring yourself that life can wait for a few minutes until you catch your breath.

The problem, of course, is that you've been breathing junk. What we're suggesting, if you want to quit smoking, is that you kick the tobacco but keep the actual habit of dosed, breath-focused self-care. In other words, the trick is to ditch the smoke but keep the smoke break and to learn to *smoke air*. And that's entirely doable; you've been practicing breath awareness for years. We'll help you rebuild a smoke-free body on the breath-focused platform that you have built with the help of your smoking. You haven't smoked in vain!

Smoking as Coping through Ritual

Smoking, like any repetitive behavior, is a ritual. Rituals are emotionally stabilizing because they provide a sense of predictability. When you participate in a familiar routine, you have a feeling that you know what's going on, so you begin to calm down and relax. Life is uncertain, and people escape into rituals to create illusions of simple predictability. That's normal. So, smoking, as a ritual, is just another psychological oasis, a behavioral sequence that cues the mind to relax. With time and repetition, not only does the smoking behavior go on autopilot but so does your own internal reaction to it. Relaxation becomes conditioned and automatic. You invest seven minutes of the body's health in return for about as much time in your mind's well-being. It would seem like an ideal exchange, except for such existentially and financially cheaper coping rituals as *just breathing*.

Smoking as Socializing

As a behavior, smoking is a social lubricant. Striking a match is an entirely legitimate pretext for striking up a conversation with a total stranger. Smoking, in this day and age of smoker ostracism, is a way to make lasting social bonds. For a moment, just consider that age-old gesture of goodwill of offering a fellow smoker a cigarette or a light! When we quoted Edward Bulwer-Lytton, we left out the rest of the quote: "The [person] who smokes thinks like a sage *and acts like a Samaritan*" [italics ours] (quoted in Kuntz 1997, 82). There's something intensely primordial about this Promethean give-and-take among random members of a human tribe.

Finally, for some, smoking-related socialization is all the socialization they get. There are legions of socially phobic, socially isolated smokers who huddle together, braving the elements of their designated smoking gulags, motivated by a shared smoking moment as much as by the smoke itself.

Smoking as Aesthetic

The smoking-cessation community seems to have a misguided notion that smoking is unattractive, which is way off mark. Of course, smoking is attractive to some people, actually to many people. That's why smoking has been such an integral element of the movie screen and fashion. To claim that smoking is unattractive is to misunderstand the smoking audience. Smokers love smoking, not just for its coping value but also for its aesthetic. No, we aren't talking about the cigarette butts, the ashes on your jacket, the stained fingers, or the possibly foul breath. We are talking about smoking itself. There is indeed some archetypal pyrotechnic magic to it. After all, as a civilization we began with the mastery of fire. Then, take the smoke itself. The undulating, mesmerizing, existentially poignant transience of this substance is a fitting metaphor for the ghost of our own ephemeral presence. Finally, smoke makes the dynamics of the breath visible, the caress of the drag on the mouth, the cooling brush of air through the fjords of the mouth and nasal cavities, the billowing force of the exhalation, and the cloud of the unknowing of it all.

Certainly, we are not trying to sell you a habit of smoking. You already have it. We are just acknowledging the reality of this unique habit that has held the West in its trance since 1492 and the world at large for ages. And we are in good company with all kinds of literary and creative types who dared to acknowledge the reality of smoking for what it is. Our goal at this point is simple: to get on the same page as you are by acknowledging smoking for what it is. Calling smoking a filthy habit, as some smoking-cessation enthusiasts rush to do, is to, once again, miss the forest for the trees. Smoking, for those who smoke, was, is, and will be an aesthetic experience. Acknowledging it as such allows us to open ourselves to the necessity of finding beauty elsewhere.

Viewing smoking as an unattractive, irrational behavior sells a lot of treatment but doesn't necessarily produce any substantive clinical outcomes. Smoking, as we clinically see it, isn't foul or self-destructive. It is but one of many coping choices, with its own set of pros and cons—nothing more and nothing less. But let us take the rest of this analysis one point at a time. Let us now talk about what smoking isn't.

Smoking Isn't a Disease

This obvious and self-evident point, strangely, tends to ruffle a lot of feathers in the substance-use treatment community and among users of various substances. There are many different ways of arguing that smoking is not a disease, but we don't want to bore you with clinical, conceptual, and philosophical technicalities. Instead, we'd like to offer you the quickest way we know of to dispel this psychologically toxic myth (that smoking is a disease). It's a simple syllogism, a three-punch logical uppercut. Prepare your jaw:

1. You cannot quit an actual disease (such as cancer or even the flu) on demand or by choice.

2. You can quit smoking on demand or by choice anytime.

3. Therefore, smoking is not a disease.

That wasn't so bad, was it? We hope not.

Smoking Isn't the Worst Coping Option

Coping exists on a range, from seeing a therapist (sophisticated coping) to displacing your rage onto a random driver in traffic after a hard day at work (primitive coping). Smoking, in our assessment, is somewhere in between. In his 2007 article "One Last Cigarette Before the Firing Squad? Certainly Not!" Paul Johnson, a columnist for the *Spectator*, writes: "I suspect smoking is one of those indulgences which, bad in themselves, prevent human beings from doing worse." Exactly so. Indeed, you could do a lot worse than to cope by smoking tobacco. Face it: as a smoker, you've found a self-sufficient way to regulate how you feel. You get burned; you light up. Burned again? Light up again. It works well enough, or you wouldn't be doing it. Can you do better than that? Of course you can!

Should you feel bad about the coping you've done so far? Absolutely not; you've done the best you could, and that's something to acknowledge and celebrate. Your smoking was and is a partial coping success, not a coping failure. Time to build on that!

Smoking Isn't an Enemy

Epidemiologists and public-health zealots seem to have a misguided notion that smoking is an enemy—maybe to them, but not to smokers. We find it profoundly ironic that many of the smoking-cessation self-help books and pamphlets immediately lose their audience by misrepresenting the deep, sentimental relationship between a smoker and smoking. Take, for example, the opener from the combatively titled tome *Kicking Butts: Quit Smoking and Take Charge of Your Health*, from the American Cancer Society (2010, 1). The very first paragraph of the introduction page is full of psychologically useless fearmongering and oversimplification: "You know cigarettes aren't good for you," the page begins in all caps, "but there's something about them that keeps you coming back. What is it that keeps you smoking? And what can help you stop? This book will help you get to know your enemy, the cigarette, and learn what it takes to defeat it. After you're armed with this knowledge, you'll have one of the most important days in your life, the day you quit smoking." Oh, boy! There's so much psychological toxicity here. Let's itemize:

1. As a smoker, you don't think of cigarettes as an enemy; you think of them as a friend. Anyone who doesn't see this misunderstands the nature of your predicament.

2. Sure, you know cigarettes are bad for you, for your *bodily* health; but you also know that you aren't just your body. You know, from daily experience, that smoking has been an effective coping habit, instrumental in maintaining your *mental* health.

3. "What keeps you smoking?" is the right question. The right answer is habit, not disease; mindlessness, not lack of willpower.

4. "After you're armed with knowledge…" Knowledge has nothing to do with quitting. If knowing about the health hazards of smoking

could help you quit, there would be no smokers left. Recovery isn't about knowledge; it's about "skillpower" (in the form of craving control; alternative coping; slip, lapse, and relapse prevention; self-acceptance; and other recovery maintenance skills that you will learn in this book).

5. "You'll have one of the most important days in your life, the day you quit smoking." Let's thank whoever set this unforgiving, all-or-nothing bar of success for the zero margin of error they left you with. Just imagine buying into this perfectionistic view, having a puff on or after "the most important day of your life," and then feeling like crap about yourself. Who needs that?

We get it: as a smoker, you have a strong sentimental connection to smoking, and we are not going to misrepresent it, cheapen it, or demonize it.

Smoking Isn't a Sin

There is a lot of guilt-tripping nowadays about smoking. Ignore it. Smoking is not a sin. Smoking is coping. Coping is self-care. Taking care of ourselves, the best way we know how, is what we all do. Keep doing it until you figure out how to take care of yourself more effectively. But until that smoke-free smoke break in which you smoke nothing but unfiltered Mother-Nature air, give yourself a break. You've done your best to cope. Even if it's not good enough for idealistic coping purists, we hope it's good enough for you, for now. So, keep reading, living, coping—and smoking, for now.

What Lies Ahead

It is our prediction that before too long, you will be pleasantly surprised by the wealth of experiential guidance that we have packaged into this program. In a nutshell, the program consists of the following:

1. In phase one, you will continue your smoking but begin to reduce it by loosening up the habit through a series of awareness-building

and pattern-interruption exercises. These exercises will help you use your smoking behavior to begin to break down the cues, triggers, and associations that maintain the smoking habit. At the same time, you will begin to rediscover the awesome capabilities of your own lungs for delivering pure Mother-Nature air for cost-free, healthy coping.

2. Phase two consists of intensive craving-control training and cultivation of a broad repertoire of various recovery-maintenance skills to build maximum "skillpower" for behavior change.

3. In phase three, having invested an adequate amount of time in craving control and other quit-prep skills, you will test your skills readiness and set a quit date, if abstinence is your final destination.

At all times, we will respect your right to self-determination and defer to you to decide on the final destination of your recovery efforts. What this means is that as you read on, you will have to eventually decide whether your final destination is abstinence or cutting back (harm reduction). We encourage you to take your time in reading through the next two chapters before you dive into the nuts and bolts of habit modification.

Conclusion: Upgrade Your Coping Platform

Before we go on, let us clarify one essential point. As we see it, smoking as such isn't a problem, but an attempt to solve a problem. Unfortunately, it is a highly expensive coping solution to the routine challenges of day-to-day living. Thus, while the surface-level point of the book is to help you stop or modify your smoking behavior, our deeper objective is to help you leverage maximum well-being so you can upgrade your coping software to live the life you want to live.

Chapter 2

An Unofficial Apology

The antismoking crusade was ready to grasp anything that could demonize smoking, and in 1988 the US Surgeon General declared on his own authority that smoking was an enslaving addiction and that nicotine was a drug of abuse equal to crack cocaine. On its face the statement was and is preposterous, but the media loved its capacity to conjure anxieties and to foster allegations of dark conspiracies.... No official apology or change-of-mind admissions are likely to be forthcoming, as they should.

—Gio Batta Gori, *Virtually Safe Cigarettes*

Smoking always was a bit of a hassle: you had to remember to take your cigarettes with you wherever you went, you had to make sure you had a light, and you had to have money on you to buy cigarettes. But at least you could smoke pretty much wherever you wanted. Things have changed. You've been run out of society, like a leper. Tough break. Modern-day smoking—in a society of closeted hedonists disguised as puritans—has become a game of hide-and-seek in which you, the smoker, are hunted down and corralled into a designated "smoking preserve" by guilt-tripping public-health crusades. While Gio Batta Gori, the Health Policy Center epidemiologist and former tobacco-industry consultant quoted above, appears to call for an apology to the tobacco industry, we feel that the only apology necessary is owed to you, the smoker. This chapter is an offer of apology to you. We feel that you have been treated unfairly, and we wish to make amends.

Remembering the First Casualties of Antismoking Crusades

It is ironic that we know so precisely how Western smoking got its start: "On 6 November 1492, two members of Columbus's crew returned from their adventures in the interior Cuba. They reported an encounter with the natives in which they had smoked dried leaves" (Gilman and Xun 2004, 9). We know the names of these first two Western smokers: Luis de Torres and Rodrigo de Xerez. We know what happened to at least one of them:

> Rodrigo de Xerez packed some tobacco for the return voyage… and by the time he set foot again in his hometown of Ayamonte, in southwestern Spain, he was hooked…. As the only man in town, and probably on the entire European landmass, so addicted, he was [an] offensive…sight to his friends and neighbors…. The Spaniards could not understand what had happened to dear old Rodrigo on that voyage to the Indies…. They decided after a while…de Xerez had become possessed by the devil on his journey…. The citizens of Ayamonte discussed the matter among themselves and decided there was but one course to take: report the evildoer to the Inquisition…. The Inquisitors, as was their way, showed little mercy" (Burns 2007, 19).

As you can see, antismoking crusades are as old as Western smoking itself.

So, let us take a moment to remember Rodrigo de Xerez, the first documented casualty of misunderstanding around smoking. And while we are at it, let us also remember countless smokers all around the world who suffered for their coping choices. Let us remember Russian smokers, who, under seventeenth-century czar Michael Feodorovich, were "whipped with leather thongs until bloody," had their noses slit, and were either exiled or beheaded (ibid., 41). Let us pay tribute to Turkish smokers, who were hunted down and beheaded on the spot in sting operations by seventeenth-century health zealot Murad the Cruel (ibid.). Let us bow our heads for the smokers in China and Japan who were similarly executed or had their property confiscated. Let us atone for the Hindustan smokers, under Mogul Jahangir, who had "their lips slit so that a pipe would never again rest comfortably between them" (ibid., 42), and for Middle East smokers, who, under Shah Abbas, had molten lead poured down their throats for smoking in public. Let us, once and for all, recognize that smoking crusades achieve nothing but extremism, social stigmatization, and cruelty. We apologize for this unfortunate history of punishing fellow human beings who happened to make different coping choices than we did.

Thank You for Your Tax Support

In the book *Tobacco and Smoking: Opposing Viewpoints*, A. O. Kime (2008, 85) notes: "[S]tates are infringing on human rights by singling out a minority for higher taxes. Flush with victory over the tobacco companies, the states then began another attack, this time on the smokers themselves, by increasing taxes on tobacco to a punishing degree." As a smoker, you have been financially scapegoated. You see, "the states have turned smokers into taxpaying captives," and in case you didn't realize, this kind of "unequal taxation amounts to subjugation" (ibid., 87). Indeed, "smokers in some states pay more in taxes on cigarettes than in state income taxes, which is a polite way of saying smokers are forced to pay twice as much in state taxes as nonsmokers" (Bast 2008, 95). With all this in mind, we'd like to apologize on behalf of the country for this financial persecution of your personal coping choice.

Yes, You Have the Right to Smoke

Constitutionally, you have the right to smoke. Smoking is but one of an infinite number of ways in which a human mind tries to take care of itself. Thus, smoking is but one way to pursue well-being. In the United States you happen to have a constitutional right to do so. Just because smoking is hazardous to your physical health doesn't mean it should be illegal. David Hudson Jr., author of *Smoking Bans*, aptly writes (2004, 47), "Many legal activities in society are dangerous, including riding a motorcycle, skydiving, eating fatty foods, and even working too hard.... Some people believe that state restrictions on smoking amount to a form of 'legal paternalism' that infringes on the fundamental right to liberty enshrined in the Declaration of Independence." We apologize for our society's continued attempts at prohibition-style public-health policies. We apologize for these misguided and myopic attempts to take away your personal freedom.

You Are Not a Menace to Nonsmokers

John Stuart Mill wrote in 1859 (21–22): "The only purpose for which power can be rightfully exercised over any member of a civilized community against his will is to prevent harm to others. His own good, either physical or moral, is not a sufficient warrant." What this means is that you are entirely within your communal rights to do whatever you wish to your own health as long as it doesn't harm the health of others. This point, of course, brings the issue of so-called secondhand smoke into focus. In case you didn't know, experts don't agree on the issue of secondhand smoke. For example, David Hudson Jr. (2004, 47) writes: "The EPA study on secondhand smoke is questionable.... The case against secondhand smoke... has been questionable. Some studies have found little, if any, statistical association between secondhand smoke and lung cancer. A federal judge ruled the Environmental Protection Agency's 1993 report classifying secondhand smoke as a carcinogen was deeply flawed." Hudson concludes: "[T]he push for smoking bans infringes on individual freedom of choice." Whether or not secondhand smoke is dangerous, one thing is clear: society has crossed the line in suggesting that you are a menace to society. So, once again, we apologize: in your attempt at self-care, you never meant to hurt anyone, and it is simply inappropriate for us, as a society, to keep harassing you as if you were evil. You aren't.

No, of Course, You Are Not a Child

We also wish to apologize to you for the patronizing way in which the antismoking crusade tried to squeeze "big tobacco" at your psychological expense. You see, in an attempt to make big tobacco pay, the litigators and public-health wonks tried to blame inanimate tobacco for your smoking habit. In his online article "Smoking Right and Responsibility," Jeffrey Schaler (1997) writes: "Tobacco caused them to smoke, they claim, as if tobacco had a will of its own.... This doublespeak contradicts the scientific evidence: smokers quit all the time—when it is important for them to do so." Elsewhere he adds: "The price of one's freedom in a free society is responsibility for the consequences of one's actions.... We cannot increase freedom by decreasing personal responsibility. That's the road to serfdom."

You see, using the disease model, antismoking crusaders have psychologically sold you out by suggesting that you are not responsible for your smoking habit. By convincing judges and juries, TV audiences, and smokers themselves that *tobacco made you do it*, these misguided do-gooders have belittled your sense of autonomy and doubted your capacity for self-determination. Of course, you aren't a child; you can read warning labels, so you know perfectly well that smoking is dangerous to your health. Of course, nobody holds a gun to your head and demands that you smoke. So, we apologize for all this patronizing silliness: it is you who developed a smoking habit, and it will have to be you who quits this habit. You know it, we know it, big tobacco knows it, and every reasonable mind knows it. We, once again, apologize to you for yet another misguided attempt to rope you in as exhibit A of collateral damage. We are sorry that both the culture at large and the treatment community tried to sell you on the idea that you are a powerless child who is incapable of self-determination. You gave us way too much benefit of the doubt when we asked you to surrender your will (with our half-baked disease-model conceptualizations). You were never powerless in the first place.

You Are Not Irrational

Finally, we would like to apologize for treating you like an idiot. To see what we mean, consider the following opening paragraph by none other than the former surgeon general, Dr. C. Everett Koop, in the foreword of *7 Steps to a Smoke-Free Life* (1998, v), by Edwin Fisher Jr.: "When you think about it, smoking is a strange habit: setting fire to something you then put in your mouth, breathing into your lungs the pungent smoke from chopped-up brown leaves, smoke that makes you and your house smell bad, smoke that will eventually shorten your life. It doesn't seem to be something that most thoughtful adults would choose to do." How's that for a first-page welcome from the former surgeon general? Dr. Koop seems to think that you are a thoughtless child (as opposed to a "thoughtful adult") who plays dangerous games with fire and stinks up his home. Nice bedside manner, Doc!

Just because Dr. Koop doesn't get it doesn't mean you are a kook. The same disrespectful tone jumps out of every other book. The authors of *The Smoking Puzzle* (Sloan, Smith, and Taylor 2003, 25) make essentially the same point but with slightly more finesse: "Smoking is an especially hard choice to align with rational behavior." The message here: smoking is irrational, and so are you, the smoker. What is irrational is the failure to understand the most basic axiom of human behavior: if a behavior is chosen, it is because there is a perceived benefit, which is the very rationale behind it. A behavior with a rationale behind it is a rational behavior; is it not?

So, once again, we wish to apologize to you, the smoker, for society's continued failure to appreciate the very real reasons behind your smoking. You are not an idiot, and we are sorry that we, as a culture and a treatment community, insinuated that you were. Just because you haven't yet developed reasons to quit smoking doesn't mean that you didn't have your reasons to start smoking and that you don't have your reasons to continue smoking. Our cultural failure to see that is what's irrational.

Conclusion: Quit to Stand Up for Yourself

One thing is painfully clear: there will be an official apology from neither the despicable "big tobacco" nor the righteously zealous "big recovery." The reality is that, as a smoker, you are a member of the new underclass. Unfortunately, antismoking crusades have become antismoker crusades, and it is highly unlikely that this psychologically toxic cultural climate will change anytime soon. What this means is that you will continue to pay extra taxes, you will continue to pay the salaries of public-health wonks who built political careers by demonizing your coping choices, and you will continue to be constitutionally disenfranchised. As we see it, your best option to stand up for yourself is to quit smoking, thus removing yourself from this artificially constructed underclass.

Chapter 3

Skip the Drive-Through and Sit Down

The popular concept among behavioral therapists is that
no time is better than the present to take action against an
addictive habit. In theory, it sounds right. But the cold
light of reality presents a different picture. I am convinced
that there is a tremendous advantage in a well-prepared,
preemptive attack against the smoking habit.

—Dr. Balasa Prasad, *Stop Smoking for Good*

Smoking is a hard habit to break. What makes this seemingly simple behavior so difficult to quit is the sheer amount of conditioning that goes into installing the habit. "Smoking is a highly overlearned behavior"; if you smoke a pack a day, you take an average of 160 puffs per day (Antonuccio and Boutilier 2000, 238). Only breathing, walking, and eating behavior can compete with the stupefyingly high frequency of smoking behavior. Indeed, can you think of anything else you tend to do at least

160 times a day, day after day, week after week, month after month, year after year? Furthermore, smoking, as a habit, has a tremendously wide conditioning footprint. Smoking is connected to just about everything: to a whole gamut of emotions; to a variety of places, people, and things; and to a range of activities, such as eating, thinking, reading, driving, and having sex. So, if you think of smoking as a kind of psychological cobweb, its strands are everywhere, and its triggers linger in every corner of a smoker's life. But here's the kicker: traditional smoking-cessation programs give you only about two weeks to extricate yourself from this psychologically sticky web.

Drive-Through Smoking Cessation

The standard smoking-cessation quit-date timeline is one to two weeks. Here's an example of this kind of blitzkrieg quit-date advice from the American Cancer Society publication *Kicking Butts* (2010, 88): "Pick a quit date—about seven to fourteen days from now." Seven to fourteen days? Really?

Here's another recent example of the same: "Setting a definitive quit date...is one of the surest steps a smoker can take to promote successful quitting.... We recommend that the quit date be no more than two weeks away when set. This gives smokers adequate time for preparation without allowing too much time during which they can lose motivation to quit" (Perkins, Conklin, and Levine 2008, 83). Two weeks is "adequate time" to quit one of the toughest habits to break? If that were so, why would we see such sky-high relapse rates so early in the recovery process? "Without allowing too much time during which they can lose motivation to quit"? Wait a second; if the smoker's motivation is so frail as to expire within a couple of weeks, then why are we rushing people into the batting cage of post-cessation cravings?

Here's another example. In 1996 the Agency for Health Care Policy and Research recommended "at least four to seven treatment sessions lasting at least twenty to thirty minutes" (quoted in Brigham 1998, 244). Seriously? Between eighty minutes and three and one half hours to override one of the most overconditioned coping behaviors? What are *these* people smoking? Why the rush?

Okay, let's do some math; maybe we are missing something. Let's just see what you can possibly accomplish in three weeks of preparation for a quit date. First of all, we have to shave exactly a third of that time right off the bat—for sleeping. So, all of a sudden the three weeks become two weeks (twenty-one days minus seven days equals fourteen days). Now, subtract another week's worth of time, since most people spend an average of eight hours a day working. So, we are down to one week's worth of potential prep time. How are you going to spend it? Maybe, just maybe, you'll log a few hours with some kind of therapist in a face-to-face training. Maybe, just maybe, you'll spend a few hours reading over some supplementary materials. And maybe, just maybe, you'll be diligent enough to spend a few hours practicing craving-control skills (if you've been lucky enough to be introduced to them). So, and we are being optimistic here, you might spend a day's worth of actual prep time—a day of prep against years of massive conditioning! Who are we kidding with this? No wonder most people in smoking-cessation programs don't stand a chance of succeeding. Clearly, a day's worth of prep time—heck, even a full week of prep time—is not enough to combat the massive inertia of the smoking habit. It is simply clinically naive to expect any lasting results with so little training.

So, to sum up, we have a major clinical beef with this two-weeks-to-launch standard of care. First, this isn't treatment, but a drive-through hookup for a patch or pill. The timeline is premature and arbitrary. Second, this kind of approach gets in the way of rapport, since the two-weeks-to-launch smoking-cessation providers don't seem to trust you, the smoker, with your motivation and seem to wish to nail you down with some kind of verbal "pinky promise" contract that you'll quit. We've seen this silliness firsthand in our training during feel-good group-quit ceremonies. Third, in our analysis, the current two-weeks-to-launch quit date has the stampeding impatience of an antismoking crusade. What's our solution to this drive-through quit-date approach? A mindful sit-down.

When to Quit: Whenever You Are Skills Ready

If you've tried to quit before, your past smoking-cessation failures say absolutely nothing about your potential for success in the future. Our guess is that you lapsed and relapsed because you were dramatically underprepared. So, how soon should you quit? Whenever you are ready, of course—but not just motivationally ready, skills ready! Let us explain.

Motivational Readiness Isn't Skills Readiness

In trying to make sense of this two-weeks-to-launch nonsense, we believe that both clinicians and smokers confuse motivational readiness with skills readiness. It's one thing to want something badly but an entirely different thing to know how to get it. Say you are getting ready to be married. You set a date for the wedding—in two weeks. You are unambiguously in love and have a very particular vision for the wedding. You want to marry under the wide-open sky, Druid style. So, here it is, the morning of the wedding; you are all laced up in your wedding dress, and it's raining cats and dogs—a dilemma. On one hand, you want to proceed with the wedding; your motivation is high at all times. On the other hand, with the weather as it is, you don't want to get soaked and ruin the event. What do you do? As inconvenient as it may be to all the parties involved, you just might have to postpone the date and try it again. How come? Well, because, as motivated as you are, you don't have a backup plan for rainy weather.

It's the same with smoking: say you are gung ho as heck to quit because you are sick and tired of being sick and tired, and all that motivational jazz. Good for you. But here's the question: what will you do when it starts raining triggers? Rely on your nicotine patch? Sip some lemonade? Chew a toothpick? White-knuckle it? One of these methods might work on your best day, but what about on your worst day or even just a not-so-good day? What happens to your willpower when you're stressed out and tired, and all you want to do is smoke?

Skillpower, Not Willpower

The point is that to quit smoking, you need more than willpower; you have to have recovery "skillpower." What this skillpower is about and how to develop it is a matter of the next few chapters. It is, however, important at this moment to understand this: naked motivation is not enough. As motivationally ready as you might be to up and quit all this smoking stuff today, the plain fact is that you are not ready. Could you try to prove us wrong? Sure. Quitting, as Mark Twain famously noted, is easy; it's staying quit that's hard. Could you still prove us wrong and quit on sheer willpower? Of course you can. We'll readily grant you, the mind is a powerful thing. Greater things have been accomplished on nothing but grit and grin. But here's our guess: if you are reading this, you already gave your willpower a try. This time, make it easy on yourself: bank on skillpower, not willpower.

Mindfulness = Skillpower

Habits are automatic behaviors and, as such, are mindless. When you engage in a habitual behavior like smoking, it often happens without thinking. You might have an urge, reach for the pack, pull out a cigarette, and light up without ever having a conscious thought to smoke.

Since habits are mindless behaviors, cultivating the skill of mindfulness is important for combating or changing habits. According to addiction researchers Sarah Bowen and Alan Marlatt (2009), the use of mindfulness may help smokers to combat urges "by heightening awareness of craving and habitual reactions, and providing new skills to cope with urges to smoke."

Preliminary research studies are demonstrating the effects of mindfulness practice for quitting smoking. Such studies suggest that using mindfulness-meditation practices changes smokers' responses to urges (ibid.) and is associated with not only abstinence from smoking but also decreased feelings of distress among quitters (Davis et al. 2007).

Our program uses mindfulness skillpower in four ways. First, we use process mindfulness (mindfulness of the smoking process) to awaken the smoking "zombie" with the help of awareness-building and pattern-interruption smoking meditations. We then use mindfulness-based, breath-focused craving-control training to arm you with no-nonsense, foolproof skills for maintaining your recovery after you quit smoking. Third, for the smoker who is interested in just cutting back as part of a harm-reduction approach, we use process mindfulness and mindfulness-based craving control to help you leverage more out of less as you cut back your daily smoking ration. Finally, whether you are quitting altogether or just cutting back, we will help you see how to transition your breath-focused infrastructure of self-care that you have built with the help of smoking into a platform of breath-focused meditation and contemplation.

Skillpower = Neuroplasticity

Habitual behaviors like smoking create neural pathways in the brain. Like ruts in a road, these pathways become deeply ingrained over time, so that you naturally follow them and engage in the habitual behavior without thinking. Just as the wheels of a car naturally fall into and follow ruts, your brain circuits continue to follow the neural pathways that previous repetitive behaviors established. The good news is that brains have something called *neuroplasticity*, which is the ability to build new pathways even after years of following the same old ruts. Essentially, neuroplasticity is what allows the brain to learn new habits. But as with repairing old roads, changing your neural pathways takes time and requires the repetition of new, alternative behaviors to create new paths for your brain to follow.

As psychologist Donald Hebb first noted in 1949 (70), "[A]ny two cells or systems of cells that are repeatedly active at the same time will tend to become 'associated,' so that activity in one facilitates activity in the other." In other words, neurons that fire together wire together. After years of smoking, your neural pathways are wired so that you experience strong, repetitive urges to smoke, followed by the habitual response of smoking. Our program is designed to rewire that process so that you respond to urges to smoke by using craving-control skills. Eventually, this process rewires your brain so that you have a new response to cravings, a response that helps you quit and stay quit. For all intents and purposes, when we speak of skillpower, we are speaking of neuroplasticity. But it takes time and practice to develop.

Once again, recognize the following basic fact about how habits modify the brain: unlike computers, change in the mind's "software" (or "mindware") changes the underlying brain "hardware." Habit formation is not an act of willpower, but a process of cultivating new brain behavior patterns. You've been operating on smoking mindware, and your brain's hardware reflects that. By learning how to smoke air (how to use craving-control skillpower), you are, in a manner of speaking, laying down new neural tracks for your post-smoking life. By coupling the urge to smoke with mindfulness-based, breath-focused craving control, you are wiring your desire to smoke with your desire to be smoke free.

Conclusion: Sit Down

There is a Russian custom: before you head out on a journey, sit down. So, skip the drive-through and sit down, smoker. Scratch your head, catch your breath, and think it through. Solid preparation and timing are everything. So, how much prep time do you specifically need? This question is impossible to answer without knowing the specifics of who you are—impossible for us, that is, but not for you. In the chapters to come, we detail the skill set that constitutes smoking-cessation know-how and offer you a systematic program of skills training. We also offer you ideas on how to test your skills readiness *before* you quit (not after!). What all this means is that you can keep on smoking until you are skills ready to quit. But here's the kicker: you won't be just smoking and practicing the skills on the side. No, you will be using your smoking to practice the very skills that will help you quit smoking. That's right: we have designed a way for you to put your smoking to very good use. Exactly how this will happen is a matter of the chapters to come, but in the meantime, allow yourself to really soak up this bit of good news. Once again, you can keep on smoking until you are skills ready to quit, and from this point on, the meaning of your smoking is fundamentally changing: your smoking, as paradoxical as it sounds, will lead to its own demise. Yes, we were clinically tricky to come up with this little scheme and are about to lay it out for you in all of its paradoxical detail. Turn the page.

Part 2

Reducing Altitude: Preparing to Quit

As a smoker for many years (we presume), you've been flying in smoking circles of blissful oblivion on a high orbit of mindlessness, way outside the surgeon general's cautionary reach, on the autopilot of habit. We hope you had a good run and enjoyed yourself. But now that you have your sights on the breathing ground below, we encourage you to gradually reduce your smoking altitude. No, we aren't talking about cutting back how much you smoke. We are talking about changing how you smoke. In this part you will have a chance to turn off smoking autopilot and fall back in love with your lungs. What for? To help you prevent a smoking-cessation nosedive. You've tried to crash-land this habit on nothing but a patch and a prayer, and you've seen it bounce right up. That's physics for you: just as everything that goes up must eventually come down, anything that comes down hard tends to go back up a little. To minimize relapse, we suggest that you burn up some of your habit energy, lose some of that chain-smoking speed, turn off autopilot, and fly this smoking habit on manual for a few weeks, down to less-turbulent skies. This gradual descent will ensure a less-bumpy ride to the ground of being and help you set up a softer, more permanent landing in the long run.

Chapter 4

Awakening the Smoking Zombie: Mind Work

The enhancement of self-awareness of every cigarette smoked
is in fact the beginning of an intervention.

—Richard Brown, *The Tobacco Dependence
Treatment Handbook*

There was a time when you didn't know how to walk; your mind figured it out, taught it to your body, and put walking on autopilot. Now your body walks without any supervision from your mind. So, what started out as conscious "mind business" became mindless "body business." It's the same with smoking: when you first started smoking, before smoking became a habit, the act of smoking involved a sense of choice and a degree of presence. When you smoked, you actually smoked: you took time to enjoy yourself; smoking meant something to you. Those days are mostly gone. As we mentioned earlier, if you are a pack-a-day smoker, you take, on average, 160 puffs a day. In other words, 160 times a day you engage in a mindless behavior. Our goal is to infuse your habit with a dose of mindfulness.

You see, once a behavior goes on autopilot, you become rigid. The mind, stuck in its own routine, becomes inflexible. Habits mesmerize the mind. After smoking for years, smoking has become mostly a mechanical, reflexive, compulsive body business. Your mind had to teach your body how to smoke, so your mind will have to unlearn this smoking behavior. To help your body quit smoking, paradoxically, you will have to relearn how to smoke mindfully. The goal of this part of the training process is to turn off smoking autopilot and to turn your mind back on, to get your mind smoking so that it can eventually help your body quit.

Waking Up the Smoking Zombie

Any mind is a hostage to its habits. The smoker's mind is in the grip of the smoking habit. Our immediate training objective is to help you start your process of self-liberation from the conditioned hold that smoking behavior patterns have had on you for years. Smoking, like any ingrained habit, is a system, a behavioral complex of mindlessness. Our goal is to wake you up from your smoking trance. How will we accomplish that? Well, we are literally going to mess with your habit a bit. We are going to take the smoking habit apart one behavior at a time. We are going to deprogram and decondition your smoking reflexes. Our aim is nothing less than to awaken the smoking zombie.

A Carton of Mindfulness

Each cigarette, if you trust advertising, promises you an unforgettable experience, but the monotony of habit filters out the experience. So, most of the time, all you get is junk air. Let's change this cost-to-benefit ratio. We have prepared a series of smoking meditations that will help you filter some mindfulness back in. Instead of rushing you to quit in two weeks, we encourage you to take the next month to do some quality habit-busting mindful smoking instead. Toward this end we've prepared a carton of mindfulness for you: 150 delightfully stimulating, pattern-interrupting, epiphany-instilling, process-focused, mindfulness-powered smoking meditations.

Smoking Meditation

In the article "Smoking Meditation" (2008), Bodhipaksa, a Scottish-born Buddhist teacher and author, shares the following anecdote about a young Buddhist monk seeking advice about his smoking:

> A young monk strolled into the office of the head monk: "Say, man. Would it, like, be okay if I smoke when I meditate?" The head monk turned pale and began quivering. When he recovered, he gave the young man a stern lecture about the sanctity of meditation. The novice listened thoughtfully and went away. A few weeks later, he returned with another question: "I'm concerned about my spiritual development. I notice that I spend a lot of time smoking. I was wondering, do you think it would be okay if when I am smoking, I practice my meditation?" The older man was overjoyed and, of course, said yes.

As did the head monk in this anecdote, we encourage you to say yes to the idea of infusing your smoking with mindfulness.

Keep Smoking

The following exercises are smoking meditations, which means that we expect you to keep smoking. Let's be clear: it's not that we want you to keep smoking. No, we simply presume that you, having understood our point about the importance of being skills ready, have decided to take your time with smoking cessation prep work and, therefore, are still smoking. Ultimately, of course, it is your choice to up and quit at any point, if that's what you wish to do. That's your business; if you are dying to take a short-cut, then take it—Godspeed. Our aim, however, is to offer you a systematic and skills-based approach to this challenging task of quitting.

So, what can you expect? Learn from Bodhipaksa (2008) again:

> When I was teaching meditation at the University of Montana, I had a student, called Connie, who was very concerned about her smoking habit...so I suggested that she really pay attention to the sensations and mental patterns that arose each time she was smoking a cigarette. It seemed like a long shot, but it was all I had.

She reported that after taking up this suggestion, she was smoking a lot less. It took her longer to smoke each cigarette, and she was less likely to light up again immediately after finishing one ciggie.

Sometimes awakening the smoking zombie is enough. Both of us have seen similar results in our own practices: merely removing the automatization from the habit can lead to abstinence. There is, indeed, a chance—small or great, who knows?—that one of the following experiential exercises might trigger a life-changing epiphany, and you'll quit smoking on a dime, once and for all. Sudden, epiphany-triggered change of this sort happens all the time. So, don't rush to rule it out. If you get lucky like that, if you notice that something fundamentally changes in you, and you feel that you are "done" with smoking, congrats—but don't slam the book shut yet. Just skip the rest of this chapter.

What Do You Do in the Meantime?

Here's one more point before you roll up your self-help sleeves: as you practice turning your mind on, we encourage you to keep reading the book. As mentioned, the idea, for now, is to wake up the smoking zombie. This, of course, won't take much time. So, keep reading the book while doing the smoking meditations. Think of this chapter as awareness-building, pattern-interrupting homework to go along with your readings. The next chapter offers you a few more exercises to try, so feel free to mix and combine the exercises from this chapter and the next—and keep reading. The objective is to get you through all the exercises in the next two chapters before you get to chapter 8, a rubber-to-the-pavement moment of the next training phase.

Awareness-Building, Pattern-Interrupting Prep Work

The goal is simple: take the next month to awaken the smoking zombie. What follows is a monthlong supply of over 150 smoking meditations.

Your daily objective is to try all five recommended awareness-building, pattern-interrupting experiences. Approach these exercises as meditative play. Consider each exercise to be an investment in mindfulness. Feel free to reuse the exercises you like, but avoid developing favorites. Comfort, the cousin of habit, is counterproductive at this point. What we want is to muck up the process. So, change is the name of the game here. Keep your mind limber and your smoking hands guessing. So, here you go: time to get your mind smoking.

Day 1

Change Hands

Smoking is like walking. Start your smoking day from the wrong side of the bed; that is, switch hands. If you always smoke with your right hand, today smoke with your left hand to change the process. If you always smoke with your left hand, change to the right, even if it feels wrong. Try to remember to smoke with your nonsmoking hand all day today.

Just Witness

Sometime today, light a cigarette, and without taking a drag, set it aside and let it burn all the way. Think of it as incense. Sit and watch the smoke weave a story of the coming change. Notice the glowworm of fire crawl up the stem of the cigarette, like a slow-burning fuse. Enjoy the scent. Enjoy the sight. If you feel an overwhelming craving afterward, then smoke, of course. Why "of course"? Because you are still a smoker, because you haven't quit yet, because you are not skills ready to quit yet. So, if you feel like smoking, do; if you don't, don't. Make a conscious choice.

Puff 'n' Om

Om (or *aum*) is an ancient Eastern chant, mantra, incantation. The sound is said to consist of three different phonemes ("a," "u," and "m") and to symbolize birth, life, and death. Find an online video or audio example to get an idea of what this incantation sounds like. First, try an "om" sound. Inhale, pause, and exhale with an "om." Practice this for a minute or two. Now, light a cigarette, inhale, and exhale an "om" (along with the cigarette smoke). Lean into it: in, smoke; out, "om." Try to remember to do this throughout the day: each time you smoke, try at least one "om" per cigarette. At some point today, try to "puff 'n' om" an entire cigarette from beginning to end. As you puff 'n' om, meditate on the birth, life, and death of this smoking habit. There was a time in the past when you began smoking; the habit was born. You are still smoking, and the habit is still alive. But just as your lungs empty out the tobacco smoke to their own hum, you know that your mind is beginning to wave a final good-bye to the smoking habit. So, as you "om" out yet another cloud of unknowing, know this: habits, just like everything else, have a life cycle. Puff and hum for a while as you witness this habit dissolve in the presence of your mind. And, of course, enjoy the sound of your lungs!

Candle-Lighting

Chances are, your typical way of lighting a cigarette involves an initial drag. Practice lighting a cigarette like a candle—without the initial drag—say, off the stove, the match, or the lighter. Experiment with lighting your cigarettes by candle throughout the day today: as you smoke, if possible, "candle-light" the cigarette without the assistance of your mouth, and then smoke, if you feel like it. You will need this bit of expertise in chapter 8, during craving-control combat training.

Smoking Koan

In Buddhist training, a *koan* is a question that is designed to frustrate the logical mind. The goal of the koan is to close the mouth and open the mind. In the days to come, we'll provide you with a few smoking koans. Note that these are pseudo-koans, meaning that neither of us has the Zen authority to claim that these questions are anything more than just questions. But then you are not training to be a Buddhist monk. As you ponder these questions, embrace the ambiguity. If your mind goes blank (as you chew on these questions), leave it blank. There is no right or wrong answer. Here, asking the question matters far more than trying to find the answer.

So, here's the first smoking koan for you to consider today: *What is nonsmoking?* If you have to smoke on it, do.

Deal Yourself a Hand

You don't necessarily have to do this exercise today, but it will prepare you for a later experience. Begin to collect empty cigarette packs, and cut out the fronts and backs to make a deck of playing cards. A typical deck has fifty-two cards. If you smoke a pack a day, you get to save two playing cards (front and back) a day. With this in mind, you'll have a full deck by day 26, which is roughly the end of this prep phase. As you collect the cutouts, use a black marker to mark them as if they were playing cards. It's important to draw the card marks right on the outer design sides (*not* on the inner or blank sides). Once you gather a full deck, get someone to play a few card games with you. Notice how the significance of these designs begins to fade out of your mind. Recognize that these designs and symbols have no independent meaning without you. *You* are the meaning maker. The meaning isn't in the pieces of paper, but in your mind. The designs have the meaning that you assign to them. They can mean "smoking" or "playing." When it comes to matters of meaning, meaning is the hand that you deal to yourself. So, play the hand that you choose to deal, not the one that's been dealt to you by tobacco marketing. Ask yourself today: *Am I playing to win, or am I playing to lose?*

Day 2

Change How You Enlighten

Smoking is pyrotechnics: the cigarette is a fuse, your lungs a bomb of plea-sure and worry. Today's objective is to change how you set yourself on fire. Make time today to get a new lighter, a lighter you wouldn't intuitively use. For example, if you are into classy metal lighters, get a cheap plastic lighter with a cheesy theme. If you prefer a minimalist, slick, urban look, get something gaudy or camouflaged. Show some behavioral plasticity: pick the wrong color of plastic; if you don't like yellow, get yellow; if you like white, get black. The bottom line: undermine the seamless mindlessness of your lighting choices. Set out a charge of change. Startle the smoking zombie into wakening. Change how you enlighten this smoking habit of yours.

Here's a tip: if your finances allow, buy a dozen or so different lighters and keep rotating them throughout the day today and in the weeks to come. If you light with matches, try a lighter, if only for a day. If you never use matches, get a box of them (in addition to new lighters) and light up with a match a few times today and in the weeks to come.

Just Smoke

Zen trainers tend to instruct: when you eat, just eat; when you walk, just walk. The idea is to commit to the present, to pledge allegiance to the here and now of your life, whatever you happen to be doing. Today, when you smoke, just smoke. Kill the TV, set the coffee aside, break away from work; in other words, avoid multitasking by mixing smoking with either work or pleasure. Just smoke. Enjoy it while you still do.

Exhale a Battle Cry

Maybe you have heard the U.S. Army battle cry, "Hooah!" If you haven't, look it up (find an online video or audio example of it and study it). "Hooah" is a shout of confidence. When you are challenged with an order, you say it to convey, "Done!" Now, as you smoke your next few cigarettes today, try it as you exhale. So, as you exhale the smoke, let out a confident smoking-cessation "Hooah!" At some point today, try this battle cry each and every time you exhale, for the entire duration of one cigarette. Enjoy the sound of your lungs!

Unchain Your Chain-Smoking

Sometime today, perhaps when you get home from work, tie a leftover pack of cigarettes to your wrist with a long shoelace and drag it around until it's time to go to bed. Make sure the shoelace is long enough for you to conveniently put the pack away in a pocket, if you have one. Notice the pack pop out of nowhere as you raise your hands or try to go about your domestic life. Ponder this inconvenience. Let yourself be chained, if only for one evening. Notice the relief with which you sever the umbilical cord of this habit at the end of the day. Savor the freedom as you cut the tie.

Smoking Koan

First, review the introduction to smoking koans (from "Day 1"). Then here's a smoking koan for you to ponder today: *Who filters the mind?*

Day 3

Change Brands

Smoking is a marriage to a brand. A brand is ownership. Break your bonds. Un-brand yourself. Dare to be disloyal for a day. Reclaim your smoking sovereignty: you are free to inhale any smoke you want. Dare to have an affair with a different brand. Change your brand to change your mind today. Buy a pack of something unfamiliar today and smoke the new brand instead of your favorite.

Waste Half

Light a cigarette and wait till it's half gone. Then smoke what's left. Try this a few times today. Ponder what you are wasting and what you are conserving. Let the dollars and cents pinch your mind awake. Watch the smoke of mindlessness dissipate.

Tuvan Throat Singing

Find an online video or audio example of Tuvan throat singing. Then try it as you smoke your next few cigarettes. Exhale the smoke as you let out a gargling, throaty roar. Enjoy the sound of your lungs!

Puff Dynamics

Back in the late 1970s, researchers used "miniature flowmeters" that were "actually incorporated into the cigarette" to study *puff dynamics*. They noted that most smokers "reduce their puff volume after the first three or four" puffs and that "under conditions of stress, both puff duration and puff interval were shortened" (Thornton 1978, 394). As you smoke today, take note of these puff dynamics. Pay attention to how your "puff volume" varies in the course of smoking any given cigarette. Do you indeed begin with deeper puffs and later render them more shallow? Do you tend to take quicker and shallower puffs when you feel stressed? Is there a difference in your puff dynamics depending on whether you are tense or relaxed when you begin smoking? Smoke on that to infuse your smoking behavior with a dose of mindfulness.

Smoking Koan

Smoke and ponder this koan: *What's the price of one breath?*

Day 4

Change Timing

Smoking is timing. Ruin it. Throughout the day today, allow yourself to smoke when you don't feel like it, and if you can, avoid smoking when you feel like smoking. Go off phase, off the smoking rhythm. Be late, be early, or be off base. Learn from what happens.

Shred a Cigarette

Find a shredder, tuck in your tie or any jewelry to get it out of the way, and shred a few unlit cigarettes. Allow yourself to enjoy this simple fun. You might want to tear off the filter first (unless you have an industrial-strength shredder). Let your hands do something different, something utterly unfamiliar, if not blasphemous, with these all-too-familiar objects. If you are up to it, allow yourself to get carried away with this: shred the entire pack, one cigarette at a time. Alternatively, remember to shred at least one cigarette in the next several days. Imbue this moment with any meaning you choose. Contemplate the experience.

Now, we realize that we are asking you, in a sense, to burn money. At about five dollars a pack, a cigarette costs one quarter. Can you afford to waste a quarter or more a day? Of course you can! What do you think you've been doing over your smoking career if not burning five-dollar bills, one day at a time? If it helps, find some consolation in the following concept: each quarter you waste buys you back about seven minutes of your life (Mackay, Eriksen, and Shafey 2006). Not a shabby conversion rate with some value added in the form of mindfulness, eh?

Exhale a Dzogchen "Ah"

Dzogchen is a form of ancient Tibetan Buddhism in which the "ah" mantra, also known as "sky breath," is traditionally practiced in the morning, although you can use it at any time of day. Here's what Lama Surya Das (2005, 41–42) has to say about this mantra:

> I find that stopping in the midst of a busy trip to simply take a deep breath and exhale with a great releasing "ah" can perforate the solidity and claustrophobia of an intense day, letting the fresh air of spirit and awareness blow through. To chant the "ah" mantra, take a deep breath, and on your exhalation, open your eyes and mouth wide; raise your gaze; and chant a resounding, relieving "ahhhh" as far as you can go.

In this smoking meditation we invite you to stop "in the midst of" your smoking in order *to* "perforate" the mindlessness of smoking-related breathing with this simple awakening mantra. As you exhale the smoke of your next several cigarettes, let out a powerful, tension-releasing dzogchen "ah." Empty out the mindlessness of smoking time and again, until you hear your lungs hiss in this powerful gesture of momentary awareness. You can try it just once for each and every cigarette you smoke today, or you can try to "ah" your way through a whole cigarette, exhaling your smoking mindlessness from start to finish. Also, try to close your eyes as you inhale the smoke and open them, with an upward gaze, in sync with the "ah" as you billow out the mindlessness of smoking. Enjoy the sound of your lungs!

Mind Rinse

Get a pocket-sized bottle of mouthwash. As you smoke today, whenever you remember, rinse your mouth before you smoke. Note how this changes your experience of smoking. And, if you wish, also rinse your mouth after you smoke. Notice how this rinsing procedure changes your smoking mind.

Smoking Koan

Smoke and ponder this koan: *Is smoking the mind's habit or the body's?*

Day 5

Change Your Waste-Management Practices

Smoking creates material waste (ashes, filters, matches). Each smoker has a particular waste-management method. Change how you manage your smoking waste today. If you generally use an ashtray, put it away and solve this waste-management problem in real time. Aim to come up with different waste-management solutions for each cigarette (a paper cup, a bottle cap, a banana peel, and so on). If you don't use an ashtray, then fashion one and use it throughout the day. Allow yourself to witness the accumulating evidence of your smoking habit: notice the growing assembly of ashes and cigarette butts. Witness your smoking "footprint."

Wet Job

There is nothing as disappointing as a wet pack of smokes. Disappoint yourself. Do the blasphemous: take the pack you have on hand and hold it under your kitchen faucet. If you feel like smoking, open another pack, or go buy some more. If you cannot summon enough heart to "do in" a whole pack, wet a handful of cigarettes. Is this silly? Yes. Is it mind provoking? We think so; after all, how can you not grow from doing something that feels so counterintuitive? Dare to try. And remember that when it comes to smoking, wasting and saving are but two sides of the same coin, so it's all in how you see it. What should you do with the wet pack? Trash it!

Cough 'n' Puff

Smoking is memory. Remember your first cig? As you smoke today, at some point after you light up, re-create your first historical puff: cough it out. That's right: as you light up and take your first drag, reenact your first encounter with smoke. Recall how you almost gagged. Go down the behavioral-sensory memory lane; act out the memory. Cough 'n' puff your way through one whole cigarette. Ponder the sound of this memory.

Refrigerate a Pack

If you use smoking as a kind of appetite-suppressing, zero-calorie snack, then to break the pattern, exaggerate this point. Put a pack of cigarettes in the fridge and leave it there for a day. This way, as you open the fridge throughout the day, you'll be slightly startled and unambiguously faced with this ingenious dynamic of smoking and weight management in your life. On some level, of course, the cigarette pack will seem out of place in the fridge, but on another level, having it there will make a certain kind of sense. After all, if you've smoked in the past to avoid eating, then a cigarette pack in the fridge is not unlike a diet-soda can in the fridge that may help you bypass a meal. So, stick a spare cigarette pack in the fridge in the morning in order to defrost the associations of your mind. What gives? Try it. Don't be afraid to provoke your mind!

Smoking Koan

Smoke and ponder this koan: *Am I still a smoker in between cigarettes?*

Bizarre Quellazaire

A *quellazaire*, a cigarette holder, used to be an indispensable fashion accessory for high-society smokers. These cigarette holders came in four different lengths: opera length, theatre length, dinner length, and, of course, cocktail length. Quellazaires put up to twenty inches' worth of distance between class-conscious lips and the boiler-room soot of the cigarette ashes, betraying that bourgeois ambivalence about the pastimes of the masses. Wouldn't it be nice to try to get into these nuanced states of mind with your own quellazaire? Maybe. No, we aren't suggesting that you go hunting for these absurd vintage implements. Not at all. We'll take the lowly DIY approach to it. Unless you have a roach clip somewhere in your smoking vicinity, find a pair of tweezers, pliers, or chopsticks, and try smoking your next two or three cigarettes with some distance between you and that oh-so-proletarian smoke. Allow yourself an air of class-conscious, grotesque disdain toward the object of your consumption: *I can't believe I am smoking this! So, since I absolutely must, I must absolutely distance myself from this utterly uncouth, I dare say, stink!*

Day 6

Feeling Check

In the 1970s H. J. Eysenck and Kieron O'Connor (1979, 147), of the University of Psychiatry in London, postulated what now seems obvious, that "the major incentive for smoking is constituted by the physiological and psychological effects of nicotine," and found that these effects were, in fact, "twofold" and "contradictory": "people smoke because they are bored and wish to raise their level of arousal, while on the other hand, people smoke because they are tense and overaroused, and wish to reduce their level of arousal." As you get ready to smoke today, right before you smoke, ask yourself, *Am I overaroused or underaroused? Do I wish to up my level of arousal or tamp it down?* Jot the answers on the pack with an up or down arrow, or with a plus or minus sign. So, if you want to up your level of arousal, mark the pack with a plus sign or an upward arrow; if you are trying to calm down and reduce your level of arousal, mark the pack with a minus sign or downward arrow. In other words, before you smoke, do a "feeling check."

Change Fingers

There are all kinds of different ways to hold a cigarette. First, notice how you hold yours. Do you always hold your cigarette this way? If not, how do your fingers change their hold, and why? Throughout the day today, consciously change the way your fingers hold a cigarette. Try a few different holds as you smoke today. For example, try the "roach hold," between your thumb and forefinger, and ponder why your hold has such a hold on you.

Time a Smoke

Time a smoke. Get your watch ready, and start the timer as you light the cig. No need to rush. It's business as usual. Note the time when you are done. Write down the duration of the experience on the back of the pack. Repeat this practice a few times throughout the day to get the average. Ponder what accounts for variability.

Whistle 'n' Puff

As you smoke today, at some point whistle as you exhale the smoke. Try it once or twice. Try to whistle 'n' puff through an entire cigarette. Enjoy the sound of your lungs!

Smoking Koan

Smoke and ponder this koan: *Am I sleep-smoking right now?*

Day 7

Change Your Lip Grip

The lip grip is one of those smoking-behavior subtleties that goes entirely unnoticed until your lips numb out on Novocain after a trip to the dentist's office. As you smoke your next several cigarettes today, notice your default lip-grip position. Notice if the cigarette "lands" in the same spot between your lips or if it widely travels around your mouth. Notice if you pout your lips forward to accommodate the butt or if you clench the filter in your teeth for hands-off smoking. Study this aspect of your unconscious behavior to bring it into the habit-changing limelight of self-awareness. And change it.

Try the James Dean lip grip. You've probably seen one of those iconic pictures of James Dean on a Harley in front of the Brooklyn Bridge, looking elegantly gaunt with a cigarette hanging off his left-lower lip. Next time you smoke, toss in a bit of that James Dean attitude. Shift the cigarette into the corner of your mouth. Let your face acquire a bit of a menacing scowl. Study this interplay of facial grimace and mood. Notice how readily your mind follows the direction of the face. Ponder this intriguing connection between facial behavior and feeling when smoking.

Try the wild-rover lip grip. You've probably seen one of these manic-faced smokers with a cigarette wildly roving from corner to corner. Yes, it's cartoonish and even silly. But all this silliness is grist for the habit-changing mill. So, as you smoke today, try it out: let the cigarette travel around the span of your lips (from left to right and back) a few times. Notice the comic tension of this action.

Try the chomping-at-the-bit lip grip. Next time you smoke, allow yourself to chomp down on the filter a few times. Pinch the cigarette in between your teeth like a cigar while you smoke it from start to finish. It's important to resist your temptation to default to your regular (unconscious) lip grip. Chomp at the bit of your smoking habit.

Try the dead-center lip grip. Next time you smoke, center the cigarette plumb in the middle of your mouth, and make sure to smoke it straight from the dead center of your mouth. Notice yourself feeling somewhat decentered by this extra mind effort. Notice the temptation to just let yourself smoke mindlessly, as you usually do. But also notice a certain kind of centering presence emerge: here you are, awkward yet mindfully present. Notice this paradox of presence: whenever you go off autopilot, the routine-bound body rebels, but the freedom-loving mind ultimately benefits.

Earplugs

Take out two cigarettes. Cut off the filters. Peel off the yellow filter paper and use the cotton pieces to gently plug your ears. Have a significant other who doesn't smoke tell you, "I am concerned about your smoking. I don't want to lose you before I absolutely have to." With your ears plugged with cigarette butts, struggle to hear this person.

Help a Cigarette

Time a cigarette. Light it (without the initial drag), set it down, and time how long it burns, without your "smoking assistance." Then, help a cigarette burn by smoking it. Time the duration of your assistance. Ponder the difference you made.

Quick Smoke

Recall one of the earlier exercises, when you timed the duration of an average smoke. Let's build on that data. Now that you know how long, on average, it takes you to smoke a cigarette, try to rush it. Try to beat the time. Try to set a record of smoking efficiency. Smoke at top speed. Get focused. Eliminate any distractions and smoke. Ready? Set. Go!

Slow Smoke

You probably saw this one coming, eh? Now, have a slow smoke. Try to prolong a smoke. Explore all the different options that you have to slow down a smoke. Ponder what is within your control. What can you manipulate to slow down this experience? Does the burn rate of the cigarette depend on the frequency and depth of your puffs? Not sure? Then explore!

Day 8

Change Posture

Smoking comes with postures: sitting postures, pacing postures, leaning postures. What's yours? Study your smoking posture and try to change it throughout the day. For example, if you smoke sitting down, try standing a few times. If you tend to smoke leaning on a wall, try squatting. If you smoke sitting with your legs crossed and your smoking elbow resting on your knee, with an air of bohemian distance from the hubbub of the world, try crossing your legs differently than you usually do, or go for a walk with your cigarette. The bottom line is to reposition yourself for change!

Smoke One and Witness the Other

Get two cigarettes and light both. Light the first one as you would usually light a cigarette that you plan to smoke. Light the other one off a stove or a match as you would light incense. Smoke one as you witness the other. Ponder this: it's the same object with two entirely different uses. Not profound enough? It doesn't have to be, as long as it is different enough. Try this today to create another precedent of change-priming difference.

Smoke a Pacifier

You'll probably think this next smoking meditation is a little weird. It is. We hope that by now you are beginning to appreciate the "crazy wisdom" of these smoking experiments. And, here's a heads-up: it's going to get even weirder as we go along. But it's all for a good cause, so here's an exercise for a truly fearless mind. Worry not: we won't ask you to jump out of a plane. But we will ask you to dive into the somewhat regressive abyss of your past, mind first. Here's what we mean. Get a pacifier and nurse it for a few minutes as if you were smoking it: stick it in your mouth, take it out, repeat. While you are at it, meditate on the basic inescapable fact that smoking is a pacifier. Ask yourself, *What does smoking pacify in me? What anxiety does it quell? What am I worried about? Can smoking solve these issues? If not, what can?*

Add to the Burden

If you happen to have wrist weights, try smoking with them on at some point today. So, before you light up, add to the burden: put the wrist weights on and then smoke. As soon as you are finished smoking, take them off. Feel the relief!

Smoking Koan

Smoke and ponder this koan: *Why am I paying for air?*

Day 9

Change the Setting

Smoking comes with its own environment. Today we challenge you to change the setting. If you have a certain place where you like to smoke, change it. If you smoke inside your home, try a new corner of the house, a different chair, a different place. Try the same tactic with outside smoking: if you smoke in front of your house, walk away a few feet or maybe go around the building, if that's an option. As you smoke today, consciously displace your smoking body to move your smoking mind to awareness.

One Drag

At some point today, when you light up to smoke, try subsisting on just one drag. "Candle-light" the cigarette: off a match or the stove, without taking the initial hit. Look at it, as if it were your very last one; enjoy the sight, smell the smoke, and, when you're ready, take one conscious, mindful drag. As you inhale the smoke, close your eyes, feel the smoke work through the fjords of your body and mind, and feel it search its way out of you. That's it, for this moment. You are done, for now. Either put out the cigarette or let it burn away. There's nothing else to do in this moment; it's just an opportunity for self-awareness.

Tap as You Smoke

As you smoke today, at some point make a conscious choice to tap your foot once every time you take a drag. Don't worry about why just yet. The meaning will be made clear as you read on.

Smoke on It

At some point today as you smoke, ponder the following fact: "Every cigarette takes seven minutes off a smoker's life" (Mackay, Eriksen, and Shafey 2006, 34).

Smoking Koan

Smoke and ponder this koan: *Is smoking hot or cool?*

Day 10

Finger Interference

As you light up today, make a point to put a pen in between your non-smoking fingers. Build in this nuisance to awaken your smoking mind. Trip up your autopilot to lose your smoking balance. Notice your mind coming back online as you stumble. Repeat this practice throughout the day.

Chin Up

As you smoke today, at some point try to raise your chin up high as you exhale the smoke. Make it look grotesque with that art-deco, onward- and forward-leaning optimism, or as if you were the wave-breaking figurehead on the bow of a Viking ship. The "why" doesn't matter. The "how" (of the resulting mindfulness) does. Face the immediacy of the smoking moment!

Dot Down a Puff

Remember the tapping exercise from day 9? This is a variation on the same theme. As you smoke today, each time you take a puff, put down a dot (with a pen or pencil) on the pack. There's no need to count them or total them initially. Just go through the experience. Notice the emerging sense of presence as you attend to each and every puff. This practice of dotting down the puffs will help you later.

Let It Blow

Slice a handful of cigarettes open. Gather the loose tobacco into an empty cigarette pack, and step outside. See if you can find an elevated place, a scenic spot. Pour the tobacco out onto your palms, take a deep breath, and blow the tobacco back into the world it came from. Return it to the wild reality of our shared origins. Let a smile stretch your face as you welcome the opening in your mind. And worry not: tobacco is biodegradable, just as you are.

Smoking Koan

Smoke and ponder this koan: *How long is life?*

Day 11

Smoke Solo

Smoke alone today. During your smoke breaks at work, make a conscious choice to avoid company by finding some solitude and smoking all by yourself, without any social distractions. If you share your home with someone who smokes as well, just for today, avoid smoking in company even at home. Notice the difference and ponder it.

Pop Bubbles

Get a large piece of bubble wrap. Buy it if you need to. Light a cigarette. As you smoke it, in between the drags, pop the air pockets of the bubble wrap one at a time. Do it all day whenever you smoke, until the entire sheet of bubble wrap is gone. Meditate on the experience. Meditate on your hesitation to try it.

Cooling the Hands of the Habit

When you want to smoke, it's as though your hands were on fire: the body, with mindless efficiency, executes a series of microbehaviors. Here's a chance to literally cool off the hands of your habit. Brace for it: it's a strange exercise, but if you are still with us, today you will smoke solo most of the time, so it's a great day to try this. Before you smoke your next cigarette at home, prepare a bowl with cold water. Light the cigarette and place your usual smoking hand into the bowl. Submerge your entire wrist. Notice the urgency to hurry and finish the cigarette so you can end this strangeness. Be ready for some other unexpected insights. Repeat to explore further.

Pick a Leaf

Tobacco, as you know, starts as a leaf. Like all living things, tobacco plants bask in the same sun as you do and draw sustenance from the same earth as you do. On the evolutionary tree of life, if you go way, way back, you and tobacco are cousins. Pick any leaf—not necessarily a tobacco leaf—from a flower, a bush, or a tree, and slide it behind the plastic of the cigarette-pack wrapper. Carry this leaf in your pack throughout the day, and when you smoke, allow yourself a moment of compassion: the tobacco you are burning was once a leaf itself, absorbing the light of the amazing, mind-boggling sun over your head, and transforming its energy so the plant could grow. Recognize that life is not a commodity, not yours, not anyone else's. Live free and don't sell out!

Smoking Koan

Smoke and ponder this koan: *What is entering, and what is leaving?*

Day 12

Burn the Past

As you open a new pack today, before you smoke or do any of the following daily smoking meditations, write down all of your reasons for quitting—*on the cigarettes*. Write the names of the people that you quit for—*on* the cigarettes. Write the dates of your past attempts to quit and the methods that you used—*on* the cigarettes. Twenty cigarettes is plenty of paper to document it all. As you plow through the pack in the course of the day, watch the words burn, and ponder how they all go up in smoke. But don't despair. Allow yourself to believe that it will be different this time. Allow yourself to recognize that it already is different. After all, here you are, not impulsively jumping into quitting, but taking your time to methodically prepare. Here you are smoking mindfully, with an emerging plan in your mind and without beating yourself up—smoking contemplatively, smoking philosophically; who would have thought it possible?

Change How You Exhale

Smoking isn't just inhalation; it's also exhalation. First, study how you usually exhale (straight out; from the corner of your mouth; sifting the smoke through your teeth, through pursed lips, through rounded lips?). Then, as you smoke today, consciously change how you exhale. Try a different method with each cigarette. And remember to stick with the chosen exhalation method through the duration of any given lit cigarette. Exhale the mindlessness of the habit!

Flick Contest

There's nothing like being able to flick a cigarette butt with a carefree gesture. No, littering isn't nice, nor is it legal. However, this exercise isn't about littering, but about the sheer simple joy of flicking a butt. Today you get to consciously indulge this little pleasure. Save a day's worth of cigarette butts, and in the sanctity of your own home, flick some butts. Draw a line on the floor or mark a spot on the ground in your backyard, and compete with yourself. How far can you flick a butt? Five feet, twelve feet, beyond the horizon? Play with this. See if you can flick a butt out of your sight.

Count the Puffs

At some point today as you smoke, mark a dot on the pack for each puff of a single cigarette, and when you are done, count up the number of puffs per cigarette. Try this a few times to get your own puff-per-cig average. This practice will help you later with craving-control training.

Smoking Koan

Smoke and ponder this koan: *When I am full of smoke, what am I empty of?*

Day 13

Savor to Mourn

Chances are you like to smoke. Chances are you've thought of cigarettes as your faithful, trusted friend, a reassuring "blankie" of sorts that you drag around all day. Life is like that: we all cling to objects because they can't abandon us. Soon, but no sooner than when you are ready, you will begin the process of letting go of this particular form of self-care, just as, at some point, you let go of that blankie. But for now, hold on to it tightly. Hug a pack of cigarettes. Go ahead. No, we are not kidding you or mocking you. You love what you love, and we are not judging. Sure, you can take our words to mean that we aren't really sincere—that we are, in fact, sarcastic in subtext. We aren't. But, for crying out loud, let go of thoughts of what *we* mean by this. Right now it's just you reading this page; we might already have left this planet. So, it's just you, always you—and so far, your faithful cigarettes. So, take a moment to acknowledge this connection.

That's what we humans do; we develop sentimental connections with safety objects. And that's entirely normal. We all need our pacifiers. So, hug the pack, and when you smoke the next time, make a conscious choice to hold on to the smoke as well. Let today, for no particular reason, be the day you allow yourself to mourn, in advance, your eventual parting with this reassuring habit. So, as you smoke today, whenever you remember, right after you inhale, hold on to the smoke for a conscious moment: *Here it is, a moment of my smoking life.* We know you know, but nevertheless here's a cliché for you: all things eventually come to an end. To savor is to mourn. Meditate on this.

Gloves On

As you smoke today, when you care to remember, put your gloves on. Literally. Try your winter gloves. Try your driving gloves (if you happen to have some). Try your gardening and work gloves. Try to add a meditative layer of textured distance between your hands and tobacco. Let your habit mind get out of touch!

The Great Smoking Escape

As you smoke today, once or twice, notice the glow of the cigarette. Turn it toward you and notice the encroaching advance of the black-and-red fire at its tip. You've been playing "catch me if you can" with this little bomb fuse for how long now? Allow yourself to marvel at this: here you are, handling fire and, hopefully, still beating the odds of who knows what! As you watch the cigarette burn its way toward your body, allow yourself to appreciate this strange play with fire in which—thousands of times!— you managed to escape with your fingers unburned. Meditate on this escape-artist routine of yours. Yes, you keep getting away with this. How marvelous in a way! How daring and fortunate! Celebrate your great luck. But, smoking Houdini that you are, also ponder whether your luck has an expiration date. Please accept our apologies; we don't mean to bum you out and leave you hanging on an ominous note. That's not the point. The point is this basic question, from you to you: *Have I had enough of this game? Should I perhaps quit while I am ahead?* Ponder this as you watch the fiery tip of the cigarette inch its way toward your body. Will it ever catch up?

Smoke on It

At some point today as you smoke, ponder: "Twenty-five years of life expectancy [is what] a typical pack-a-day smoker loses" (Brigham 1998, 244).

Smoking Koan

Smoke and ponder this koan: *If I started smoking due to peer pressure, should I also quit due to peer pressure?*

Day 14

Straighten Your Arm

As you smoke today, at all times do your best to remember to try to keep your arm totally straight. Of course, bend it stiffly when you take a puff, but once you're done with the puff, re-extend your arm. If you are sitting and smoking, let your smoking arm hang straight down by your side. The "why" doesn't matter, but the "how" of mindfulness does. Try it to leverage presence.

Blown Away

This exercise isn't a scare tactic—not at all—just a humorous and hopefully provocative experience. Get a birthday cake and adorn it with the number of cigarettes that correspond to the number of years you have smoked. Insert the cigarettes into the cake by their filters. Now, light the cigarettes and allow yourself to be blown away by this little production. Marvel at this smoldering mess! Now, one by one, pull out each cigarette, flip it over, and extinguish it by burying it in the icing of the cake. Feel free to smoke or not during this strange acknowledgment of what is. Tune in to the ambiguity of this moment: is this a celebration or a parting? You'll just have to smoke and see.

Make Rings

Blow some rings today. Wait till it's dark outside, or just kill the lights for better contrast. Light up, lie down, and blow some rings. Enjoy the prolonged exhalation of your pursed lips. Feel the breeze of the outgoing air as you decorate the atmosphere. Enjoy!

Lie to Yourself

False promises aren't just broken; they are constantly renewed. Take a pen and write on the paper cylinder of the cigarette: "I will quit today." Don't mean it, of course. You know you are not skills ready. It's just a simulation, a mind-opening game, so play along. So, open a pack, and write this lie on every cigarette. As you smoke today, watch your lie burn and ponder how you will ever know when you are finally ready to mean it.

Smoking Koan

Smoke and ponder this koan: *If I quit smoking, should I let the tobacco industry know that I did?*

Day 15

Snap a Band

Get a rubber band and put it on your wrist. Wear it all day. As you smoke, each and every time you take a puff, snap the band. Now, make sure you get a loose rubber band. An argument could be made (although it's not our argument) that you are already hurting yourself each and every time you take a puff, so there is no need to hurt yourself twice with a rubber-band snap. This rubber-band snap is not there to make smoking painful, but to make it more mindful. There is a world of difference between the two.

Oh, the Pleasure!

At some point today, right after you light up, we'd like for you to say out loud, or at least under your breath but with most sincere gusto, "Oh, the irreplaceable pleasure! What will I ever do without you?" Sure, it sounds corny. The fact is, the very sentiment is corny. But that's the jig of it: you mean it every time you panic at the thought of quitting. So, spend a day meaning it. Enjoy the theatrical drama of this! Shoot a video and upload it to a website, if you dare, or e-mail it to us at smokefreesmokebreak @gmail.com (and we'll upload it to our book website). Smoke right into the camera as you histrionically lament the pain of a possible separation.

Clap Hands

What's the sound of one smoking hand clapping? Find out. Find something hilarious to watch. Light up, and the first time you crack up, clap your smoking hands, with the cigarette in between your fingers.

Meet Your Guardian Angel

The filter is the holy of holies of the cigarette, the very technology of illusion that gives us a sense of safety as we smoke. Desecrate the holy: clip off the filter. Unwrap it to see the high-tech magic that keeps the toxins outside and so cleverly filters in the spirit of pacification. Meet the guardian angel that's been keeping you safe all these years.

Smoking Koan

Smoke and ponder this koan: *Who will quit for me: gum, patch, pill?*

Day 16

Change the Bump

Notice your specific way of bumping off ashes. How do you do it? Do you flick the cigarette butt from below, with your thumb? Do you touch the edge of the ashtray with the tip of the cigarette to knock off the ash? Explore. And, as your smoking day progresses, do it with consciousness. Bump the habit mind off its throne of mindlessness!

Black Out the Warning

Printing the surgeon general's warning about the risks of smoking on cigarette packs is a mixed proposition. Sure, the warning is important. But let's face it: who's paying attention anymore? The mind is marvelous at habituating—for example, ignoring what is always there. So, today, as you start a new pack, black out the warning with a marker. Notice your mind, all of a sudden, noticing the black box—ironic, eh?

Lie about Smoking

We don't know you, of course, but you've probably found yourself, at times, downplaying your smoking, particularly after you have tried to quit, when "harassed" about your recovery progress by your significant others. Try this (and don't bother trying to make sense of it). With a black marker, write on your cigarette pack: "These aren't my cigarettes." On another pack (that you plan to smoke), write: "I have never smoked." On yet another pack (if you have a carton somewhere near), write: "I don't know what these are." On yet another pack, write: "They call them 'cigarettes,' but I have no idea what they mean by that." On a different pack, write: "One day I will learn how to smoke, develop it into a habit, and then try to quit a few times until I succeed." Lie to yourself about smoking to crack yourself up when you handle these packs in the days to come. Notice the humor and the enlightening confusion of these memos to yourself. Organize your insights.

Dispel the Mystery

Sometimes you feel as if you could kill for a cigarette, though we hope that's an exaggeration. Sometimes you feel as if you couldn't live without smoking and as if a cigarette were a friend, a therapist, or maybe even a lover. Get inside this magic. Dissect a cigarette. See where all this power is emanating from. Solve the mystery of this ancient mist once and for all. Take a cigarette and place it on a chopping board. Slice it open to see the hidden magic for yourself. If, while reading this, you sense a certain "tone" in our words, let us assure you that we are junkies for paradox. We both mean it and don't mean it. We are simultaneously sarcastic and in awe of the power of smoke. But enough about us and our attitude. Unwrap the mystery yourself.

Smoking Koan

Smoke and ponder this koan: *What's the sound of one iron lung breathing?*

Day 17

Change Your Smoking Gestures

Smoking is a highly choreographed, behaviorally nuanced habit. Get a cigarette, whether lit or not, in your hands and try out your smoking gestures. For example, you have a habit of flicking the rim of your nose with your thumb as the smoke tickles your nostrils. Or you might have a habit of touching your lips, brow, or chin with your thumb as your smoking fingers play around your face. Notice these subtleties, try them on purpose throughout the day today, and infuse your previously automatic gesture with a moment of mindfulness.

Heed Yourself!

Different people fear different things. The surgeon general's warning obviously doesn't reach every smoker's mind. Make your own warning. Get a label and write down your own fears. Stick the label over the surgeon general's warning as you start a new pack today. Notice your mind start to heed its own warnings.

Ashes to Ashes

Notice the ashes. Did you know that ashes are sterile? Ponder how you, too, if you plan to be cremated, will one day assume the same powdery lightness. As you smoke, let some ashes fall onto your nonsmoking palm. Inhale and blow the ashes off your palm! Blow this moment of self-awareness to existential smithereens! Collide with your existential angst head on! Feel the impact of mindful presence.

Measure the Caliber

If you are knowledgeable about guns, investigate the "caliber" of the cigarette you are smoking. Gauge its diameter and ponder what gun it would fit into. Ruth Mandel writes (2004, 184): "A former Soviet army officer mentioned that during his training, he was taught that the diameter of cigarettes and bullets were intentionally identical. In theory, any cigarette plant could be converted into a munitions factory." Find out for yourself the caliber of what's killing your lungs.

Smoking Koan

Smoke and ponder this koan: *What will my smoking friends say if I quit?*

Day 18

To Finish or Not to Finish

Today as you smoke, as often as you can remember before you light up, make a point to formally ask yourself, *Will I finish the cigarette or not?* Decide before you light up whether or not you plan to finish a given cigarette, and then smoke. It's very important to bear in mind that whether or not you comply with your intention is utterly irrelevant at this point. This isn't about keeping promises or following through. We absolutely don't care about that at this point. This exercise is simply about making a conscious choice on the front end. It isn't about executing that intention; it's about formulating an intention in the first place. So, make a conscious choice, take a moment for conscious planning, have a moment of intention, and then smoke. Whether you finish or not, whether you do what you planned or not, is entirely irrelevant. Just make the choice.

Scenic Smoking

If you are going to smoke outside today, say, during your lunch break at work, try to find a scenic site, somewhere with a breathtaking view. Alternatively, if it's your day off or you are at home and have time, make an event out of this. Pack just one cigarette with you and go to your scenic smoking spot, or drive there if you have to. Find a spot off the beaten path that provides some solitude, and light up.

Catch Your Own Eye

Decorate your smoking fingers today with eye-catching jewelry to catch your mind's eye. Wear something flashy, something metallic, something that will force you to notice it; perhaps the metal of your fingerwear will be a glint in your eyes with each advancing puff. If you are not comfortable with decorative jewelry, use sentimental jewelry, such as a class ring. Or use washable black marker to draw a visible dot, star, plus sign, or just a line on one of your fingers. At any rate, practice self-reflection: *Here's my hand moving toward my face with a cigarette in between my fingers; who is moving this hand, me or my autopilot?*

Rained Out

If it happens to be raining today (if not, save this idea until it rains), step out to smoke. As you huddle under an umbrella or the edge of a roof, watch the wall of raindrops come down all around you. When you are ready to end the smoking session, simply extend your hand into the rain with the burning cigarette, and wait for the rain to put it out for you. Let the rain quit your smoking for you. If you lived in water, it'd be so much easier to quit. Try this; don't just read through it as if it were a meditative vignette. It is that, of course, but just as smoking imaginary cigarettes isn't exactly the same as actually smoking, reading through all these exercises without trying them is far from the real thing. Open your mind and close the book.

Smoking Koan

Smoke and ponder this koan: *What would I pay to just up and quit for good?*

Day 19

Change Stores

Change your buying habits. Go to a different store today. If you have to, drive out of your way. Take the convenience out of the errand to infuse it with some conscious choice. Try to buy the next however-many cartons you get one at a time, each at different location. Waste a shortcut: take your mind on a detour of presence.

Finger Paint

As you smoke today, save the ashes. At the end of the day, finger paint your name on a sheet of paper with the ashes. Worry not: this isn't dirt, just a metaphor for your own finality. Contemplate this moment.

Multitask

Smoking, for many, is multitasking. We bet you can smoke and drive, smoke and type, smoke and walk, smoke and talk. Test your smoking multitasking prowess at tying shoelaces. How about juggling? How about washing dishes? Try to see. Don't just read through this; give it a go—today! Study the experience.

Pop a Sleeve

As you open a new pack today, take off the plastic sleeve and twist it shut, entrapping a bubble of air, as if it were a pocket of breathable air. Pop it!

Smoking Koan

Smoke and ponder this koan: *If Mother Teresa were alive and trying to quit, how would she go about quitting?*

Skip the Manicure

Cosmetics camouflage. Painting over stained nails is good for appearance, but the "truth" of your smoking, of course, goes unnoticed. Dare to go one week without a manicure. Let yourself see your "handiwork." The idea is not to gross you out, but to simply awaken your mind. Chances are that as you begin to point your stained fingers at your own face, you just might see yourself in the mirror of self-awareness.

Day 20

Bag It

Get a sealable plastic bag. Dump the cigarettes out of the pack into the bag, and carry this makeshift cigarette bag with you instead today. Cigarette packs are, of course, conveniently compact. The cigarette bag, however, will be a nuisance. But that's useful. Any friction you can add to your otherwise seamless, habitual smoking habit is likely to slow the momentum of your smoking behavior at least enough to let you pause for mindfulness.

Corner Yourself

Remember time-outs, where you stand in the corner facing the wall? Corner yourself today, at least once: smoke your next cigarette facing the wall. Leave yourself no way out; get boxed in. Feel the smoke reflect back toward your face in a kind of physical feedback. With nowhere else to go, here you are, your face against the wall, dead-ended. Notice where your mind takes you from here. Whenever you notice the urge to turn around, do. And as you do, allow yourself to open up to a space of possibilities in front of you.

Shadow Smoke

Shadowboxing, in a manner of speaking, is training with an imaginary opponent represented by your own shadow. Shadow smoking has nothing to do with shadows and everything to do with imagination. It's fake smoking. It's a form of pantomime in which you mimic smoking. Chances are you might have done it once or twice as a kid with a pencil or lipstick instead of a cigarette. It's time to regress: role-play an act of smoking in real time, from the first to the last puff. Shadow smoke a single "cigarette" today. Savor the process.

Sham Smoke

Take yourself through the process of smoking a real cigarette without lighting it. This is just like shadow smoking (previous exercise) but with an actual unlit cigarette. Savor the process.

Smoking Koan

Smoke and ponder this koan: *Would I still smoke if I had a conjoined twin (joined at the hip) who was a nonsmoker?*

Day 21

Choose a Smoking Path

Today, as often as you can remember before you light up, make a conscious choice to either just smoke or multitask. This isn't about following through and keeping promises; it's about having that fleeting moment of conscious consideration. Whether you just smoke or multitask is irrelevant. Just remember to have a moment of conscious choosing. After you decide, document the choice: write "JS" (for "just smoke") or "MTS" (for "multitask smoke") on the pack. Think of the moment before smoking as a crossroads of sorts: one path is that of just smoking, and the other is that of multitasking; stated differently, one path is mindful smoking (just smoking), and the other is mindless smoking (multitasking). Choose a path and accept whatever trajectory your smoking follows. Practice choosing. Choosing is a skill.

Pinch Your Nose

Unlike other human senses, the sense of smell plugs right into the emotional (*limbic*) circuits of the brain. As such, smell is a powerful trigger. At some point today, experiment with taking your nose out of this smoking business. For the next two or three cigarettes you smoke, try pinching your nose. First, pinch your nose, and then take a drag; after a brief pause, exhale through your mouth, and then notice your mouth breathing in between the puffs. Turn your nose off and on with your fingers to mind the difference.

Try a Nose Blockade

At some point today, also try applying a bit of menthol rub to the tip of your nose. Notice how the interference of this nontobacco smell plays into your overall smoking experience today. Muck up the process to leverage mindfulness. Take stock of your insights.

Dragon Breath

At some point today, try exhaling a few puffs through your nose. Check yourself in the mirror, if you have a chance. Try it in company, say, during a smoke break at work. Try opening and closing your left and right nostrils with your finger. Try it in a dimly lit room. Snap a picture of yourself doing this. Play with it.

Smoking Koan

Ponder this koan today: *What is the smell of freedom?*

Day 22

Earn a Star

Let's face it: for years you've thought of smoking as a reward. Let's make it official. Get a bunch of star stickers. Slide the sheet of star stickers behind the plastic wrapper of your cigarette pack. Each time you smoke today, give yourself a star. Right before you light up, peel off a star and stick it onto your cigarette pack. Enjoy the act of rewarding yourself.

Zoom In

Get a magnifying glass and systematically examine a cigarette. First, get two cigarettes. Light both and decide which one you will smoke and which one you will examine. Make a conscious choice. With one cigarette in the corner of your mouth and a look of inquiry in your eyes, as if you were a cross between Humphrey Bogart and Sherlock Holmes, smoke and study, smoke and study. Zoom in on the glowing embers of the cigarette. Look at the snake of smoldering smoke from the cigarette you are studying. Take a closer look at the gray, powdery ash buildup on the inert cigarette under your examination. Study the mystery.

Decorate the Pack

Decorate the heck out of the cigarette pack. Get a bunch of different stickers and markers. As you get ready for the next day, set aside the cigarette pack for tomorrow and turn it into a work of kitschy art. Why? In your mindless smoking, you probably never pay attention to the particular pack you handle; you just get it out of the carton, and that's it. Here, you have a chance to infuse the very pack of cigarettes with an artistic touch of mindfulness, which will come in handy when you smoke. Chances are you will freak out a little when you reach for your cigarette pack and pull out an absurdly ornate totem pack. We predict that this will jolt your mind into a moment of presence.

Smoking Koan

Smoke and ponder this koan: *Who smokes?*

Day 23

Chopstick Fingers

Smoke a few cigarettes with chopstick fingers. Light a cigarette and hold it with a pair of chopsticks. Play some classical music while at it, waving your hand like a conductor to the movement of the rhythm. Does it sound too crazy to try, or too enlightening not to try? Try to see which it is: crazy, enlightening, or both.

Corncob It Out

You know those little corncob forks? If you don't have a set, get one. For an evening or two when you smoke at home, use them to fish the cigs out of the pack. Why? Try it to figure out why.

Night-Vision Smoking

Wait till it's pitch dark, or just lock yourself in a lightproof room and kill the lights. Light a cigarette and use its glow as a source of illumination, as a flashlight for your body and mind as you move around this life space. Be careful not to trip and burn the place down.

Smoke in the Lotus Position

Get a flower or a blade of grass, and sit in the half-lotus position, where the left foot is placed up onto the right thigh and the right foot is tucked under the left thigh. Light a cigarette. Hold the flower or blade of grass in one hand and a burning cigarette in the other. Smoke air—that is, just breathe—until the cigarette burns out. Try this at least once. Repeat it if you like.

Smoking Koan

Smoke and ponder this koan: *Am I still a smoker when I am asleep?*

Day 24

Eye of Awareness

Paint a simple "eye" on the index fingernail of your smoking hand, and let it stand for "eye of awareness." Make it conspicuous—say, a white eye shape on a black fingernail, or vice versa. As you smoke today, notice the eye, notice yourself noticing it, and wake up. If you are not comfortable painting an eye on your fingernail, put a bandage on your index finger and draw an eye, or just write "I" on it to jar your mind into self-awareness. At any rate, notice yourself as you point at yourself.

Bandage

This is a variant of the previous exercise for women and, we guess, a modality of choice for men. Instead of painting an "eye of awareness" on your fingernail, put a fingertip bandage on both of the fingers that are involved in holding a cigarette. If you dare, go with "Hello Kitty" or "Dora the Explorer" bandages, or something outstanding enough for you to notice. And once you do (notice yourself), notice yourself noticing yourself. Enjoy the self-referencing feedback loop of awareness. Process how it changes your smoking process.

Smoking Gun

Today, as you smoke in the privacy of your home, try to smoke a few cigarettes by holding the cigarette with both hands, as if it were a gun. First, clasp your hands as if around a makeshift gun, and notice your index fingers touching each other. This is your finger hold for the cigarette. When you light up, clasp your hands as if holding a gun, with your cigarette in between your index fingers. As you take a puff and prepare to exhale, point the "handgun" outward and shoot out some smoke. Crack yourself up to crack the foundation of your smoking habit. Try it a few times and get into the role: you are a bad badass, like Dirty Harry or Lara Croft, Tomb Raider.

Smoke to Music

Download a few tracks of Gregorian chants and smoke to the mystical sound of human breathing. Hum along.

Smoking Koan

Smoke and ponder this koan: *Am I still a smoker when I am not smoking (such as in between cigarettes)?*

Day 25

Lose a Link

Whether you are chain-smoking or not, smoking itself is a behavioral chain, a series of behavioral steps seamlessly linked to a mindless sequence of smoking behavior. Take a link out of this chain. Analyze your smoking ritual; determine what is inessential and lose it. If you tap the pack, lose the tap. If you roll the cigarette in your fingers before you light it up, lose the roll. Mind the difference.

Smoke, Eat, Play

Once again, here's something totally crazy, absurd, and possibly mindfulness provoking. At some point in your smoking life today, get something yummy to eat. Then, light a cigarette, take a drag, exhale, and set the cigarette aside as it burns. As the cigarette smolders, have a bite of your favorite food, savor it, and then put the burning cigarette right into the remaining food. Break the boundaries, merging one play with another. You didn't need to smoke, but you chose to, for fun. You weren't necessarily hungry, but you chose to eat, for fun. Now, combine the two actions in the most direct way. Extravagantly and with divine flair, fuse fun with seriousness and seriousness with fun.

Make Clouds, Make Smog

If it happens to be a sunny day, full of azure sky, find a lawn or a meadow and lie on the ground, on your back. Light up and billow out clouds of smoke, using your own lungs to paint the sky. If it happens to be overcast, then step out with a cigarette and add some smoke to the cloudy sky. If it's just another humdrum day, fume a cigarette or two, adding to the smog around you. The bottom line is to rethink yourself as part of all that naturally is!

Nature Sounds

Get a few audio tracks of nature sounds. Smoke to the sounds of thunder, rain, a babbling brook, wind. Join the sound of reality.

Smoking Koan

Smoke and ponder this koan: *Who smokes, and who quits?*

Day 26

Cigarettes and Coffee

Coffee and cigarettes often go hand in hand. Let's change hands. Next time you smoke and drink coffee, swap hands. If you are in the habit of handling both items with one hand, split up the duties. Toss a monkey wrench into this little routine of yours to see that "coffee and cigarettes" doesn't quite feel the same as "cigarettes and coffee." Savor this awareness-building confusion as it deteriorates the mechanics of your smoking habit.

Smoking Twilight Zone

Self-reference is a peculiar thing. When, for example, you quote yourself (as in "As I have said before…"), who are you: the one who quotes or the one who is being quoted? You can ponder the possible philosophical depth of this question later, but for now, try this. Light two cigarettes: start smoking one, and use the smoke to blow out the other. When you successfully blow out one of the cigarettes, light it up with the help of the cigarette that is still aflame, and start smoking the newly re-lit cigarette while trying to blow out the original one. Keep going for a little while until you find yourself a bit lost in this twilight zone of smoking cessation and smoking initiation. Savor the confusion. Let it muddy up your smoking mind.

Windshield Wipers

Sit down. Light two cigarettes and rest both of your elbows on your knees or thighs so that your hands are pointing to their respective sides, as if you were in a lotus position, meditating. As you smoke, take alternating puffs from each hand, noticing how your hand movements resemble those of windshield wipers. There's no need to rush this process to keep up the pace. Just try to remember to be in the moment enough to keep the alternating sequence. Stop when you reach the halfway point of each cigarette so as to not overdo it. What's the point? Does there have to be one? It's not as though each time you smoke, you have a mindfully chosen point; or do you? If so, what is it? Take account: clean the fog from the windshield to see where you are driving this habit.

Pack It Wrong

Open a new pack, take out the cigarettes, and reinsert them wrong-side up. Whenever you get ready to smoke, the wrong side might just put you in the right state of mind. Change the polarity: from mindlessness to mindfulness.

Ambidextrous Smoking

Here is a great way to muck up the smoking process and to leverage some mindfulness. Next time you smoke, light two cigarettes at the same time, let them burn down about halfway, and then finish what remains, one hand at a time. In other words, smoke using both hands, as you would sling a pair of Peacemakers in a Wild West shoot-out, but at your usual puffing pace. Notice the kinesthetic confusion. Notice the cogs of your mindless smoking machinery come to a grinding halt. All of a sudden, your body will be disoriented a bit, and your mind wide awake. Why let the cigarettes first burn about halfway? To keep your nicotine intake to its usual dose. Try this a few times to muck up the behavioral tranquility of your smoking habit. Think of this as tossing a couple of bricks into a pond of smoking dormancy. Enjoy the sobering effect of the ensuing awareness.

Day 27

Misuse a Cigarette

Cigarettes are for smoking, right? Wrong. As you smoke today, look for nonsmoking applications for cigarettes. For example, try using one as a bookmark (in a book you don't plan to finish). Try using a cigarette as scratch paper: tear off the filter, open it, dump out the tobacco, and make a note to yourself (your choice of message). Try plugging a hole with a cigarette: tear off a filter, find a hole, and plug it. Try using a cigarette as a traction substance: instead of chalk powder, tear open a cigarette, grab some of the tobacco, and rub it on your hands to dry them for extra traction when you bench press or open a jar. Misuse tobacco to begin to end its abuse.

Arrange a Moment

Ikebana is the Japanese art of flower arrangement. As with most Asian arts, there is an accompanying meditation. If you are a gardener or happen to have some flowers in the house, pick a flower or two, and perhaps a few leaves, and insert the petals and leaves into the cigarette-pack sleeve. As you finish your current pack, move the flowers into the next pack, until they completely dry up. Let this arrangement of natural objects accompany your lungs as you both wilt.

Mouth Juggle

Get several different flavors of chewing gum. Try combining chewing gum with smoking. Notice the extra awareness as your mouth tries to juggle two different tasks. Notice the confusion of flavor as the familiar tobacco taste mingles with the different flavor of the gum.

Spice It Up

Let's build on the previous concept. The next several cigarettes you smoke, dip the tip of the filter into a bit of salt or pepper. You don't have to overdo it, of course. Just add a slightly different taste. See what your mind comes up with next.

Smoking Time Capsule

Exhale a few puffs into a rinsed soda bottle and screw the cap on. Congratulations: you have just bottled the sight and the smell of this very moment. Place this bottle where you can see it and make a commitment to hold on to it for a few years. Imagine yourself one day releasing this smoke into the wild. That'll be a moment to remember!

Day 28

Change Access

Open the pack the wrong way. Instead of scraping the thin red line with your nail, cut the pack open down the center using a knife. Embrace the possibility of cutting into a few cigarettes inside. Don't worry: they can't feel it. Ponder the associations that come up for you.

Bum a Cigarette

If you smoke, congratulations on your financial self-sufficiency. We presume that you are not charging smokes you can't afford, and therefore have avoided acquiring a huge debt from smoking. We presume you are on a pay-as-you-smoke basis. If so, once again, congrats. Now, let's exercise some humility. Go bum a cigarette. That's all. Try it a few times and ponder the experience.

Flash Code

If you are familiar with Morse code, try this. Light a cigarette, turn the lights off, and, holding the cigarette between your thumb and index finger, toggle it back and forth, using the cigarette's glow as a light signal. Signal "SOS."

Glow Lights

Ever been to a rave? If so, you know what to do. If not, read on. Light a couple of cigarettes and turn off the lights. Holding a cigarette in each hand, start making quick, swooshing, tai chi–like motions. Watch the dance of the trailing lights.

In, Health; Out, Health

Visit a gym (if your doctor allows). Put in a good workout (to the extent your health allows; there's no need to exert yourself; this isn't about trying to prove anything). After you've worked out, go outside—not to the car, not home, but right in front of the gym—and smoke a cigarette. Remember, you still smoke, so that shouldn't be a big deal. Savor the juxtaposition: in, health (in the gym); out, health (outside smoking). Contemplate the peculiar symmetry of this input-output sequence.

Day 29

Light It Wrong

You've probably seen people do this when they are discombobulated, and perhaps you have even done this. Light the wrong end of a cigarette. Yes. No need to smoke the filter, of course. Just have this moment. Feel the crumbs of tobacco leaves on your tongue. Smell the shoulder of the filter.

Connect the usually soothing moment of smoking to a feeling of being out of sorts. Set a precedent of affective mismatch: whereas you usually connect smoking to a feeling of ritualistic clarity, here set a precedent of associating smoking with confusion. In other words, instead of letting smoking signify a solution to confusion, let it represent confusion for a change.

Put a Twist on Putting Out

How do you put out the cigarette? Do you tap it down? Do you heel it? Do you "screw" it back and forth until it's out? Put a twist on how you put out a cigarette, to help yourself put a twist on how you quit smoking.

Go on Record

List three reasons why you should smoke—not three reasons why you shouldn't, but three reasons why you should; not why you do, but why you should. Restrain yourself from listing the reasons why you should quit smoking. How come? There are none. There is absolutely no reason why you *should* quit smoking. There might be some reasons why you might *want* to quit smoking, but no "shoulds." Quitting smoking is not an ethical or moral imperative; thus it's not a matter of should. You probably know what we mean, right? Remember all those times you thought to yourself *Why should I quit?* Well, change the question a bit. Ask yourself *Why should I smoke?* Go on record with yourself.

Lobby for Smoking

The fact that you smoke means that on some level, you endorse smoking as an activity. If so, why not recommend it to someone? Make a point to recommend smoking to a nonsmoker. Put on your best smoker face and say to someone, "There's something I'd like for you to try." Lay out your case. Be persuasive enough to convince yourself. Avoid minors, of course.

Community Service

Whether or not you have ever flipped cigarette butts onto the street, spend a few minutes picking up cigarette butts. Get a trash bag and a pair of gloves, and find a safe area for this bit of community service (say, a park, an empty parking lot, a school yard, or a playground). Here's the key part: if you still smoke, try smoking as you do this. Revel in the irony.

Day 30

Unfiltered Zazen

Whether or not you know how to meditate, spend a few minutes a day just sitting in a half-lotus position with an unlit cigarette in one of your hands. If you don't know how to meditate, don't bother trying. This experience has nothing to do with meditation. If you do know how to "just sit" in a meditative manner, put all that wonderful contemplative know-how aside and literally just sit there in a half-lotus position with an unlit cigarette in one of your hands. While there seems to be nothing to this, we ask that you remain open to a chance epiphany. If you feel that just sitting there with an unlit cigarette is a little too much to ask, feel free to light it up so that you can justify this strange practice of just sitting there. Don't waste any time trying to reread this section for hidden clues or meaning. Spend an authentic moment with a cigarette without doing anything. That's all there is to it: *zazen* unfiltered.

Smoke and Mirrors

Stand in front of a wall-mounted mirror. As you are looking straight at your own reflection, light a cigarette, inhale deeply and billow out a cloud of smoke toward the reflection of your face. See your face disappear. See through this habit's "smoke and mirrors." Wait for the smoke to dissipate to see your original self again.

Reflected Smoking

As you smoke your last cigarette of the day, do it in front of a mirror. Sit down, light up, and smoke. Reflect on what's going on.

Smoking Blind

Smoke your last cigarettes of the day with your eyes shut. See what it's like not to see the smoke from a cigarette. Get a glimpse of your future smoke-free life, in which you will smoke air. It will be just as now, when you are smoking with your eyes closed, but without the benefit of the smoke as evidence.

Smoking Koan

As you wrap up your change-priming phase, smoke and ponder the following koan: *What is the difference between smoking and breathing?*

Conclusion: Smoke Interrupted

The change-priming approach that you have been working on in this phase of our program is not without precedent. Back in the 1970s the Smoke Watchers suggested a pattern-interrupting, awareness-building step as part of their overall quitting program. There is a Russian saying: "Rush, and you will blush." Smoke Watchers, as with our own approach, "allowed" smokers to take their time quitting, *while smoking*, by using the very behavior of smoking as a vehicle for smoking cessation. As a result, 35 percent of people who quit using the Smoke Watchers program were still smoke free at the one-year follow-up (Schwartz 1973)! Contrast this success rate with the abysmally low one-year abstinence rates of 5 percent of the modern-day "drive-through" smoking-cessation interventions (West and Shiffman 2007; Garvey et al. 1992). While the Smoke Watchers movement demonstrated impressive outcomes, the "take your time" approach to smoking cessation has totally vanished since the 1970s, as the self-help paradigm has shifted from a process focus to an outcome focus, from mindful behavioral change to a magic-pill, quick-fix mentality. The lesson is this: take your time to interrupt your smoking mindlessness, or risk being interrupted by it after you quit.

Chapter 5

The Breath Wind of Change: Breath Work

Soon you will be in control of your breathing,
and not the other way around.

—Bill Stromberg, free diver

Your lungs are amazing! In a manner of speaking, lungs are a sail that powers your life with the wind of breath. Just like sails, lungs harness the energy of reality and make this power available for your mind's rudder to steer with. Rediscovering the beauty of your lungs is both an awareness-building and habit-modifying opportunity of this training phase. Whereas "awakening the smoking zombie" with the help of pattern interruption (chapter 4) is the mind-work portion of your smoking-cessation prep, this chapter is the *breath* work.

Get Inspired

The word "inspiration" (just like the word "spirit") stems from the Latin verb *inspirare*, which literally means "to breathe in." This is your opportunity to inspire yourself and to fall in love with your own lungs. The goal is nothing less than to learn to smoke air—that is, to breathe with satisfaction, meaning, presence, and gusto. As we see it, smoking, in its functional essence, is a form of breath-focused emotional self-regulation. Indeed, when practiced mindfully, smoking begins with a conscious inbreath and ends with a conscious outbreath, just like a breath-focused meditation. Therefore, chances are that much of what you are about to try will be fundamentally familiar to you. As a smoker, you are a kind of inhalation connoisseur. The fact is that you already know how to savor a nice, deep drag of air. What's left is to broaden your breathing repertoire.

The following breathing meditations will set the stage for craving-control training; help you crosswalk your smoking habit into a habit of contemplative, breath-focused, meditative self-care; and help you, literally, get inspired to quit. As you try the following various breathing meditations, keep awakening the smoking zombie with the exercises from chapter 4 and read on all the way through chapter 8. Give your lungs a ride or two every day. Allow yourself to get, literally, inspired by breathing unfiltered Mother-Nature air.

A Pack of Breath Work: Twenty Breathing Meditations

Following is a series of breathing meditations to incorporate into your breathing life. Enjoy your lungs!

Smoke Some Lights

Did you know that the word "lung" comes from the word "light"? For example, in Russian, the word "lung" is essentially indistinguishable from the word "light," *legkoye* and *legkie*, respectively. For a day or two, allow yourself to consider that when you are breathing air into your lungs, you are smoking "lights." Play this mind game to see what it brings about, particularly if you smoke a "light" brand. So, as you decide to light up, ask yourself, *Shall I light up, or shall I smoke some "lights"* (meaning lungs) *instead?* In other words, *Shall I light up or smoke some air?* We aren't prodding you to quit just yet. We are simply inviting you to try to remember to consciously sail your lungs for a while. Open your mind, for a few minutes, to wherever the wind turbines in your chest might take you.

Get Inspired

Realize that no breath means no creativity. "Inspiration," a technical term for inbreath, as you know, doubles as a creative mechanism. Spend a bit of time getting inspired. Just sit and breathe. Let your lungs move your mind out of its current impasse. Inspire yourself to quit.

Turn the Lights On

In his illuminating book *Buddha's Brain*, Rick Hanson (2009, 185) explains: "Oxygen is to the nervous system what gasoline is to your car.... By taking several deep breaths, you increase oxygen saturation in your blood and thus rev up your brain." Couple this with another suggestion from Hanson (ibid.): "[B]righten your mind" by "literally visualizing light." Apparently, the mere act of visualizing light "involves a surge of norepinephrine throughout the brain," a neurotransmitter that "fosters alertness" (ibid.). Take a few moments to rev up your lungs and your mind by taking deep breaths and visualizing light. Compare this lung-driven illumination of the mind with the kick you get from smoking cigarettes.

Sigh of Relief

A sigh of relief isn't just your typical outbreath. It's a prolonged outbreath. Extending the exhalation phase is a way to turbocharge the relaxing effects of your relaxation session. Hanson (2009) explains that a big inhalation requires a big exhalation, stimulating the *parasympathetic nervous system* (PNS), which is responsible for relaxation. Practice taking conscious sighs of relief. Couple some of these sighs of relief with the thought that this time you will be overprepared to quit smoking, armed with skillpower, rather than underprepared, as before, when you banked on willpower. Aaah…

Ode to the Lungs

Write an ode to the lungs in prosody or prose. Sing it or hum it. Let the hand of breath strum your vocal cords. Rest in awe.

Anapanasti

Anapanasti is a Buddhist breathing discipline that requires nothing of the student but a willingness to witness the breath exactly as it is, without any intentional manipulation of it. Find a place to sit down, and close your eyes. Give yourself permission to do nothing. After all, despite all the things you have on your plate, you have made time to do this, so do it. Begin by watching your breath. Note the up-and-down movement of your chest, the in-and-out movement of your stomach, the fleeting, breezy sensation of the air flowing in and out of your nose. Simply notice. Resist the temptation to manipulate your breath. Your lungs know how to breathe. Trust your body to find a slower and more restful pace of breathing. Just watch and observe. Let your breathing pace deepen on its own. Feel free to shift from one type of breathing sensation to another. After a while, allow yourself to acknowledge that there are two opportunities for a pause: right after you inhale, before you exhale; and right after you exhale, before you inhale. Take the latter one: allow yourself a brief moment of rest after you exhale, right before you inhale. Don't force yourself to hold your breath. Just pause for a moment. As you exhale and your stomach sinks, merely settle into a momentary pause before you inhale again. That's it. Do this for a few minutes. Try this awareness-building exercise a few times to become more attuned to the subtleties of your breathing.

Deep Breath

Now, try to consciously manipulate your breath. Close your eyes, and place one of your hands on your stomach. Notice how your hand moves up and down slightly as you inhale and exhale. Begin to take slightly deeper breaths, watching your hand move a bit higher as you inhale more deeply. Take six to twelve such abdominal breaths. If you don't notice any relaxation, keep going with more breaths until you do. That's it. Practice this a few times.

A Breath of Satisfaction

Take a few deep breaths. Notice a certain kind of emerging satisfaction. On the surface, nothing in particular seems to be happening; you are just breathing, right? Not really. You are not just breathing; you are breathing mindfully. And as your mind fills with breath awareness, as your mind becomes full of this seemingly trivial awareness, a certain indescribable satisfaction emerges. Somehow, just breathing, just living, just surviving, just being full of unfiltered Mother-Nature air feels like enough. Experiment with this; words, in this kind of matter, are often pretty useless. Find a minute to sit down, begin to take a few deep breaths, pause for a moment after you inhale, and notice the sense of fullness and release. Practice catching that fleeting yet tangible sense of satisfaction whenever you remember to do so in the next day or two.

Purifying Lotus Breath

Suffering, whether by thought, feeling, or sensation, is a stream of information that passes through the mind. Try this lotus breath exercise, taken from *The Lotus Effect* (Somov 2010a, 171), to "detox" yourself from the information that stands in the way of your current well-being. Sit down with your eyes closed. Let your chin rest on your chest. Sit like this for a few moments. Imagine yourself as a lotus flower closed up for the night, with your head as a bundle of beautiful petals resting on the stem of your neck, with your shoulders as leaves lying atop the placid surface of a pond.

Now, as you inhale, swanlike, gracefully, lift up your chin while opening your eyes. Inhale the sky of what is. Allow yourself to take it all in: all that you see, all that you hear, all that you smell. And without stopping, in one graceful, flowing motion, begin to exhale your way down to your original resting position, as you close your eyes. As you exhale what is, notice you, the one who is breathing. With your chin on your chest, pause comfortably in between breaths, catching another glimpse of the you that is in between what is and what isn't. Breathe in, breathe out. And once again, blossom into the sky of what is, lifting your chin, opening your eyes, taking it all in; and just as soon as your inbreath reaches its apex, begin to let go of everything your consciousness just touched, by exhaling all that no longer is. Repeat generously. Self-cleanse with the lotus breath until you feel informationally pure. Pilot this breath exercise for a few days to see what it does for you.

Refreshing Lotus Breath

In *Blooming of a Lotus: Guided Meditation for Achieving the Miracle of Mindfulness*, Thich Nhat Hanh (1999, 23–24) offers this: "Breathing in, I see myself as a flower. Breathing out, I feel fresh." He adds (ibid.): "We breathe in to restore the flower in us. This inbreath brings the flower in us back to life. The outbreath helps us be aware that we have the capacity to be, and are now, fresh as a flower. This awareness waters our flower; this is the practice of loving-kindness meditation toward ourselves." Take this respected teacher's advice: with your eyes closed or open, sit in self-purification; breathing in, see yourself as a lotus flower; breathing out, feel yourself cleansed.

Exhale an Impulse

Mind life is a series of thoughts and feelings, some of which bubble up to the level of an urge or an impulse. Most thoughts just come and go, but some have that action potential that eggs you on to allow them to rise to the level of behavior, to turn them it into something tangible, palpable, visible. Try witnessing and exhaling these twitches of the mind. Sit with your eyes open or closed, and notice your mind move. When you feel the urge to stop or to do something (such as to turn your head, scratch an itch, or ponder some thought further), notice the urge and symbolically exhale it.

Static Apnea Training

Bill Stromberg, a free diver, shares the following training tips, which he calls "static in bed" (2004a). Get a timer, lie down on your bed, and breathe deeply for a few minutes. When you are ready, take three deep breaths. On the last outbreath, try to empty your lungs as much as you can, and hold your breath. Notice thoughts pop in and out of your mind, and if possible, refocus on something pleasant or calm. When you experience the inhalation reflex, just notice it and keep holding your breath until you feel that you must take a breath. Check the timer. Stromberg recommends that you take a couple of fast breaths to get back to your breathing baseline and rest for a few minutes before you repeat this breath-holding exercise. He advises trying this a total of five times per training session. You don't have to; you aren't training to be a diver. Just try it to get a sense of what it's like, and if you might be interested in this kind of training, ponder how quitting smoking would turbocharge your progress.

Walking Apnea

After static apnea training, Bill Stromberg (2004b) recommends walking apnea training. Specifically, he suggests that you start walking at a normal pace, carrying a stopwatch. After walking for a while, take a deep abdominal breath and hold it as you continue walking. Stromberg suggests a pyramid-like approach to this process: first, hold your breath for fifteen seconds, then thirty, building up to your maximum breath-holding level; then gradually reduce your breath-holding time while continuing to walk. Try this and ponder how quitting smoking will turbocharge your progress.

Feel Your Breath Power

Place a candle a couple of feet away from your face and begin to take a series of deep but calm breaths. As you exhale, aim a steady stream of air through your pursed lips at the candle and try to put it out. As you blow out the candle, relight it, move it back a bit farther, and try to blow it out again with the wind power of your breath. After trying this a few times, allow yourself to think of the candle as your smoking habit, and systematically, breath by breath, blow it out.

Visualize Breath

Put a tiny bit of menthol rub on the tip of your nose, close your eyes, and spend some time mindfully breathing through your nose. Notice how the cooling sensation helps you to visualize the dynamics of the breath. Allow yourself to see a continuous stream of invigorating, cleansing mist cycling through your lungs. Enjoy.

Dzogchen "Ah"

In the previous chapter we introduced you to the Dzogchen "ah," but we misused it as a pattern-interruption device. Now try it as a bona fide breath-focused meditation. Again, here are the instructions from Lama Surya Das (2005, 41–42): "To chant the 'ah' mantra, take a deep breath, and on your exhalation, open your eyes and mouth wide; raise your gaze; and chant a resounding, relieving 'ahhhh' as far as you can go."

Exhale and Release

You may have heard of *progressive muscle relaxation* (PMR). Traditionally, it involves a stepwise process of tensing and releasing various muscle groups. PMR is a somewhat involved procedure. Here's a modified and abbreviated relaxation exercise that we use with our clients that is more portable (easier to use on the go). Clench both of your fists and hold them for a few seconds. Feel the tension build. Release the tension by opening both of your fists just as you exhale, with an exaggerated sigh of relief. Try it with just one hand. Try closing your eyes as you clench your fists, and opening your eyes as you open your fists in sync with the sigh of relief.

Breath Power

Light a candle, step back two or three feet, and try to blow it out with your breath. It might take a few attempts, but you should be able to do it. Marvel at the mysterious simplicity of this act: here you are, a distance away from a flame, too far for your hand to reach to put it out, yet capable of extinguishing it with nothing other than the power of your breath. Appreciate that your lungs always offer you the benefit of distance in that they allow you to run a safe distance away from danger. When you use them to relax, your lungs afford you a psychological distance from something upsetting. This is breath power.

Sequoia Breath

There are two living philosophies on this planet: that of flora (plants) and that of fauna (animals). Trees stand still for years, centuries, millennia of acceptance. They stay put. They grow exactly where they are, and breathe. They don't chase the greener side of the hill as we animals do. We human animals, just like all animals, chase. We search, we optimize, we run circles around ourselves. Our life is both exciting and laden with suffering. This is in the nature of the wheel, the nature of being on the go. In this breathing meditation, we invite you to get grounded. It is a biological fact that we animals (fauna) are distant cousins of plants and trees (flora). This is no metaphor. We share the same primordial, bacterial origin (Margulis and Sagan 2000). So, knowing this, stand, for once, rooted in breath. Literally, stand up, spread your legs apart a bit, straighten your back, raise your chin a bit, and spread your arms to your sides, like big, powerful branches. Open your palms and fan out your fingers; branch out into the world around you! Envision yourself as a sequoia, standing firm amid your current life circumstance, not running, not escaping, not searching, not optimizing, but in calm, millennial wisdom of accepting whatever is. Breathe with your whole body. Feel plugged in. Remain as is.

Big-Picture Breath

Sit (in a lotus position) or stand (in sequoia position). Breathe as you ponder the following. The air you are breathing has been on this planet for billions of years. It has surely powered many lungs and many lives. They have all come and gone. And now it is your turn to inhale this oxygen, to breathe this gift. That's the big picture of it all. You've been taking your breathing for granted. But it's not just breathing. It's living! So, don't just breathe; live. Let the small mind worry later about when and how you will quit smoking, but right now, let the big mind breathe with a big smile: *Thanks to breath; you are alive!* So then, celebrate your existence with breath!

Conclusion: Inhale the Wind of Change

Bill Stromberg (2004b), the free diver we quoted at the opening of this chapter, says, "Soon you will be in control of your breathing, and not the opposite way around." While he intends this advice as a tip for free-diving aspirants, we feel that his words offer exactly the kind of motivational inspiration that is bound to benefit you in your efforts to quit smoking. Some wait for a wind of change to move them; others create it themselves. Move some air—with conscious satisfaction and meaning, with balance and gusto—to feel the breeze of change in your nostrils. Rule the air!

Part 3

Destination Abstinence: Craving-Control Training

In this part of the book, we focus on getting you "skills ready" to quit for good. If you have already set your goal as harm reduction, we encourage you to keep reading rather than skip this part. How come? Cutting back, in and of itself, can be part of the eventual preparation for total abstinence. With this in mind, the craving-control training that we will discuss in this part just might come in handy one day. So, whatever your smoking destination might be, we feel that the following part is worth your while. We will first provide you with an overview of craving-control training, then offer hands-on craving-control training, and finally introduce a program of extensive craving-control practice that will allow you to take all guesswork out of this essential recovery skill set.

Chapter 6

Craving-Control Skillpower

The addiction to smoking is a problem of the mind, not of the brain.... Proponents of drug therapy...and nicotine replacement disregard the depth of dependence and the strong influence of the habit over the daily activities of the smoker.

—Dr. Balasa Prasad, *Stop Smoking for Good*

As you keep loosening the grip of the smoking habit on your mind (with the help of the smoking meditations from chapter 4) and as you keep falling in love with your lungs (with the help of the breathing meditations from chapter 5), it is time for you to begin to learn about craving control, one of the core skills of this smoking-cessation process. If, by now, you feel ready to quit, you are certainly free to try. But if you've decided to wait to quit until you are skills ready, then *for now*, keep smoking and continue reading about how to use your smoking behavior against itself.

Craving-Control Training Overview

Chapters 6 through 8 set out our craving-control training program. This chapter introduces the reasoning behind real-life (exposure-based) craving-control training and discusses how to use craving control to hijack the smoking habit. Chapter 7 will provide the specifics of mindfulness-based, breath-focused craving control, and chapter 8 will set out a program of craving-control practice. After you practice craving control for a while, you will have a chance to test your skills readiness (chapter 14).

Skillpower, Not Willpower

Imagine that you just smoked your very last cigarette. It's sheer mind-on-mind combat as you tiptoe around life as if it were a field of craving land mines. But as wise and strategic as you are about avoiding any smoking triggers, time and again you find yourself dying to have a cigarette. Unless you know how to skillfully defuse these recurring cravings, your recovery is in danger. At such moments of craving, in your gut you know that this is no time to improvise. More often than not, ex-smokers just try to white-knuckle their way through the craving on willpower. You might be able to wing it once or twice, but face it, without tried-and-true, no-nonsense, systematic craving-control know-how, you are really just flying by the seat of your pants. For most people, willpower doesn't cut it; you need craving-control "skillpower."

Cultivate a Craving-Control Reflex

We suggest that you take the guesswork out of these moments of craving. Learn an effective craving-control strategy and put it on autopilot. Overprepare rather than underprepare. Develop a foolproof craving-control reflex now, while you still smoke, to ensure your post-cessation abstinence.

What's a Craving-Control Habit?

You know how to build habits. You learned to smoke, right? Now, you need to develop a new habit, a habit of craving control. Let's begin by distinguishing a smoking habit from a craving-control habit. A smoking habit can be expressed as the following psychological sequence:

Craving → Smoking

You have a smoking habit when your craving to smoke leads you to engage in the behavior of smoking. Now, contrast this with a craving-control habit.

You have a craving control habit when, as soon as you develop a craving to smoke, you kill (defuse, control) the craving rather than satisfy it by engaging in the behavior of smoking. A craving-control habit can be diagrammed as follows:

Craving → Craving Control

A craving-control habit isn't a moment of hesitant decision making over what to do about the craving. It's not an on-the-fly search for solutions. A craving-control habit is a pattern of decisive, reflexive, overlearned, overconditioned, overrehearsed, nearly automatic craving-control actions.

Control or Be Controlled

When it comes to habit modification, it's control or be controlled. You see, cravings hijack the mind. The mind surrenders control and is compelled to comply. To fight the power of habit, you need to control the habit sequence. Here's what happens right now. As a smoker, day after day you endlessly recycle the following sequence: you develop a craving, and you satisfy it with a craving response. Craving leads to smoking. Here's how we can diagram this process:

Craving → Smoking → Craving → Smoking
(ad infinitum and ad nauseum)

Our plan is to override this smoking sequence by inserting the craving-control step. From this point on, each time you develop a craving to smoke, you will first kill the craving, and then *smoke anyway*. Notice the change in the process:

(Craving → Craving Control) → Smoking

What's the point of this activity? To reprogram your mind. Right now you are operating on smoking software: *If I have a craving to smoke, then I will* (mindlessly, reflexively, automatically) *smoke*. The new software is: *If I have a craving to smoke, first I'll kill the craving and then smoke anyway, if I consciously choose to*.

Imagine that you diligently trained like this for a while. Sooner or later you will develop a habit of noticing the craving and immediately defusing it on the spot. So, what we are trying to do here is literally condition craving control onto the very desire to smoke. We are inserting a craving-control wedge into your smoking habit, in effect overriding the smoking habit with the habit of craving control. The point of this training is to make craving control automatic, reflexive, and habitual so that you don't have to improvise in a crucial moment of craving, after you've decided to smoke your last cigarette.

A Smoking Episode Is a Craving-Control Training Opportunity

From this point on, while you are in the craving-control training phase, think of each smoking episode as a craving-control training opportunity. In the next chapter, you will learn the mindfulness-based, breath-focused craving-control method that we call "smoking air." Once armed with this craving-control technique, you will begin to practice craving control while you are still actively smoking. Each time you develop a craving to smoke, you'll first smoke air—that is, kill the craving, and then you will smoke the actual cigarette if you so choose. To clarify, we are not asking you to stop smoking yet. You are not yet skills ready. From this point on, your smoking becomes the very vehicle that will help you eventually quit smoking and stay quit.

Training by Immersion

This approach to craving-control training is immersive in nature: you are learning to lasso cravings right in the middle of Marlboro Country. There is nothing abstract, imaginary, or artificial about this approach. It's on-the-job training. It's an aggressive, pragmatic, hands-on, no-nonsense Trojan horse attack on the City of Smoking. With each successfully defused craving, you are sneaking your way into the very heart of the smoking habit and eroding it from within, breath by breath, with powerful precedents of craving control. From this point on, any smoking you do is to help you quit smoking. Savor the irony!

Plan of Attack

Here's what's ahead:

1. You will learn how to smoke air—that is, to kill the craving with a mindfulness-based, breath-focused craving-control procedure (chapter 7).

2. You will be introduced to two craving-control practice levels (of varying intensity) to make your craving control fast and effective (chapter 8).

3. You will continue with real-life, exposure-based craving-control training until you feel that you are skills ready.

4. When you pass a skills-readiness test, you will be in a position to start planning a quit date while "studying up" on recovery-maintenance skills.

Conclusion: Learn from the Past

If you look back at the last time you tried to quit, you may have a bit of willpower bravado: maybe you did slug some psychological cravings clean out of the ballpark without any of this craving-control nonsense. If so, good for you! But let's put your past successes in context. You were still fresh out of the barracks, riding that motivational high, madly fighting your way through the slog of first-time craving combat with whatever you had at your disposal (toothpicks, straws, and support meetings), improvising your way through this early-abstinence obstacle course, fleeing any temptation you could, and making very heavy use of your willpower. So, if you've tried quitting before, you know that the first couple of weeks weren't terribly awful, particularly if you were on some kind of nicotine-replacement product. That's one of the reasons smoking-cessation success rates tend to hold for a short while. The real struggle begins when you go off the patch or the gum or the pill, when your motivation to stay abstinent fades to the background as routine takes over. And that's exactly when the impromptu craving-control combat begins to fail. That's when the relapse rates skyrocket. It's like a flank attack. You rammed right through the thick of the enemy troops, but bam!—all of a sudden, there are more of them (cravings) coming at you from behind every corner. This, of course, catches you with your pants down. By this time your support people have already assumed that you have won that battle, and suddenly you find yourself alone, one on one with a series of gnawing, recurrent, often insidiously out-of-the-blue cravings. And then it dawns on you: the battle for abstinence has just begun. That's when, more than ever, you will need to call in some craving-control air support. With this in mind, your overall training goal is to make craving control your first order of smoking business so that in the weeks to come, whenever you have a craving, the first thought that should pop into your mind is *I need to defuse this craving*, rather than *I need to go smoke*. Okay, enough said. It's time to learn how to smoke air.

Chapter 7

Smoking Air

[Mindfulness] is a letting go of oneself, of letting things
happen, of not striving. This means not trying to do
something. It also means not trying not to do something.
Finally, a state beyond trying arrives.

—Dr. James Austin, *Zen and the Brain*

Smoking and breathing are nearly twins: both involve lungs; the quality of
air is the only difference. In this chapter you will learn how to combine
mindfulness-style cognitive distancing with relaxed focus on breath for an
effective craving-control skill set that we call "smoking air." Consider this
chapter to be the armory, where you get to pick up the weapon of choice:
mindfulness-based, breath-focused craving control. Chapter 8 is the shooting range. Get to know your gun, smoking-cessation soldier! (Psst, if combat metaphors don't work for you, worry not; at the end of this chapter,
we'll offer you some tips on how to customize the language of craving-
control training to suit your style.)

Not All Craving-Control Strategies Are Created Equal

There are different ways to control cravings—for example, avoidance, distraction, self-talk, and relaxation. But not all of them are created equal. Trying to avoid people, places, and things—that is, trying to control your environment to prevent cravings—is too much work and isn't always plausible. Furthermore, avoidance is running; it is fear and, thus, inevitably, is too paranoid of a life stance to enjoy. Having to distract yourself any time you get a craving is similarly taxing. Self-talk, as a craving-control strategy that tries to rein in your thoughts, fragments you into the devil on one shoulder and the angel on the other. We feel that this kind of self-splitting is too exhausting. Self-talk is a form of active resistance. It is a branch that doesn't bend under the accumulating snow.

Relaxation, as a craving-control strategy, is a step in the right direction. Relaxation, such as deep breathing, is an attempt to control your level of arousal by consciously manipulating your rate of breathing. But it's still a form of control, and all attempts at control are inherently stressful. We feel that quitting smoking is a stressful-enough change as it is, so there is no need for craving control to be yet another source of stress. And that's where the "smoking air" strategy comes in: it is enticing in its simplicity. Smoking air involves mindfulness, which takes the form of passive breath focus and passive disidentification from cravings. As such, this mindfulness-based, breath-focused craving-control strategy is a way to control by letting go of control. It is a branch that doesn't break under the accumulating snow.

Mindfulness-Based Craving Control

As a philosophy of living, mindfulness is a pledge of allegiance to the present, a pledge not to run from whatever is, a pledge to accept the interplay of the inner and the outer, in all its transient, polymorphous beauty. As a craving-control technique, mindfulness is a courageous willingness to witness the transient agony of an unsatisfied craving, a decision not to flee the inevitable but to wait it out until it flees you. As a craving-control strategy, mindfulness is what willpower wants to be but falls short of: *whole* mind power—not just the power of will, which is only a part of the total mind, but also the power of an undivided mind, the power of the mind that doesn't mind itself, the power of the kind of mind that accepts itself in its entirety. Ultimately mindfulness is the power of total self-acceptance, including cravings, doubts, and the rest of the mind junk.

Passive Attention + Disidentification

As a mind stance in general and as a craving-control method in particular, mindfulness involves two essential mechanisms: a certain kind of attention and disidentification. The following explanation is taken from *Eating the Moment* (Somov 2008, 46). *Attention* can be active or passive, that of an active observer or that of an uninvolved witness. This distinction is easy to understand through the contrast of such verbs as "to look" and "to see." "To look" implies an active visual scanning, a kind of goal-oriented visual activity. "To see" implies nothing other than a fact of visual registration. Say I lost my house keys. I would have to look for them. But in the process of looking for my house keys, I might also happen to see an old concert ticket. Mindfulness is about seeing, not looking. It is about "just" noticing and "just" witnessing without an attachment to or identification with what is being noticed and witnessed. This latter element is *disidentification*. "To identify" means to relate, to draw an equal sign between yourself and something else. When you experience a craving, there is a risk of getting lost in it, becoming overwhelmed, beginning to believe such thoughts as *I can't stand it*. And yet cravings come and go. For you to identify with something that is inherently transient is to lose your sense of self, your sense of your immutable continuity. This kind of identification with something impermanent is what imbues craving with suffering. Mindfulness allows you to recognize that a craving is but a part of the overall experience, a fleeting state of mind, not the mind itself. Mindfulness practice teaches you to realize that this thought, this feeling, this sensation (whatever it might be at any given moment) is but an object inside your mind, no more significant than a paper cup on your kitchen counter. Yes, it is a part of you, but not all of you. A craving is no more a part of your mind than a reflection of your face is a part of the mirror. And that's exactly why you can "just" notice it, "just" see it without having to stare at it.

But how do you *do* this mindfulness thing? By *not* doing it. Mindfulness, as Dr. James Austin (1999, 142) suggests, is a "state beyond trying." And a state beyond trying is a state beyond striving, beyond craving, beyond seeking, beyond reaching. That's what makes mindfulness-based craving control such a good fit for smoking cessation: it is a form of controlling by not controlling.

Mindfulness Practice

Eventually your craving-control skill set will consist of both mindfulness-style metacognitive distancing and breath focus. *Metacognitive distancing* is just "stepping back" from a thought to witness it as it passes. What follows is a brief experiential introduction to mindfulness-style presence. Take a day or two to practice these exercises. Once you get a handle on how to do this "nondoing," we will package mindfulness and breath-focused relaxation into a craving-control skill set. What about smoking? Keep smoking in the meantime. Smoking cessation will have to wait until you are skills ready.

Watching the River ("Dots" Version)

Dr. James Austin (1999), the author and neurologist mentioned earlier, called this state of effortless witnessing a "riverbank attitude." Watch your thoughts. Each time you recognize that you have a new thought event (mental image, sensation, feeling), draw a dot on a piece of paper with a pen or pencil. Set a timer for five minutes and watch your mind like this while marking dots, one after another. Remain a dispassionate observer of whatever pops into your head, as if you were sitting on a riverbank, watching boats pass by. Just watch the mind flow, the thoughts that come and pass down the stream, from right where you are, in this riverbank attitude, without getting carried downstream or getting caught up in any thought. When the time is up, look at the dots on the paper. Realize that the thoughts came and went, but you're still here. This isn't about writing down the content of each thought you have. The exercise is meant to be not a record of what you think, but an opportunity for you to learn how to step back from what you think, feel, or sense. Practice this exercise a few times a day for the next few days.

Take off the Training Wheels

Drawing dots is like having training wheels on your bicycle of mindfulness. Take mindfulness for a ride without these training wheels. Try the river-watching technique *without* jotting down a record of thoughts. Just sit and watch the mind flow. There's nothing to do, nowhere to go. You made time to be here, so be here. The world will wait. Remember that the whole business of drawing dots is just a set of training wheels on a bicycle. When you've learned to stay balanced and unperturbed by the passing thoughts, you can go for a ride without these assistive devices.

Combining Mindfulness and Breath Focus

Now, let's roll mindfulness and breath focus into a craving-control power punch. We will build on the breath work from chapter 5 (if you skipped that chapter, you might want to revisit it to spend a day or two with breathing meditations, just to prime yourself for this next step). First, we will introduce this craving-control skill set. Then, we will ask you to practice it. And, in the following chapter, we will give you ideas on how to use it to hijack your smoking habit with the help of hands-on, exposure-based, advanced craving-control training.

Smoking Air (Training-Wheels Version)

Get your pen and paper ready, light a cigarette (to trigger a craving to smoke), and set the cigarette aside. With pen and paper in hand, immediately begin to notice your mind. Namely, notice how your mind starts churning out cravings. Each and every time you notice an impulse to smoke, draw a dot on the paper, and—this is important—refocus on your breath to smoke air. Keep your eyes open so that you can see and smell the cigarette smoke. Keep noticing cravings arise and keep drawing the dots as the cravings (desires, impulses to smoke) continue. And keep smoking air by refocusing on your breath and finding satisfaction within your lungs. Let the cigarette burn out. As you smoke air, try exhaling through pursed lips as if you were exhaling smoke. Not only does exhaling through pursed lips mimic blowing out smoke, it deepens the exhalation phase of the breathing cycle and facilitates a greater relaxation effect, as if you were taking a deep sigh.

Smoking Air (Riding-Free Version)

Now, try surviving a craving without training wheels. Light a cigarette, and notice a craving arise and subside, as you refocus on your breathing by taking a puff of air, without bothering to draw dots on paper. Survive throughout the burning of the whole cigarette. Congratulate yourself on your craving-control success! Now that the cigarette has burned out, make a conscious choice to light another one and smoke it (that would be fine since you still smoke, remember?) or wait to smoke until the next time (whenever that would naturally be), if you'd like to move on with your day.

Conclusion: Climbing the Learning Curve

The rest is just a matter of climbing the learning curve. In the next chapter we will offer you ideas on how to integrate this craving-control technique into the very fabric of your daily smoking. In the meantime, choose your metaphor for craving control, using the Taoist distinctions of *yin* and *yang*. "Killing the craving"—with its implied proactive, assertive, if not slightly aggressive, stance—is a yang-style metaphor. Developers of an exposure-response prevention craving-control training program for substance use have done a great job of popularizing this combative, yang-style metaphor (Santoro, DeLetis, and Bergman 2001). "Surfing the craving wave"—with its more laid-back, dispassionate, relaxed stance—is a yin-style metaphor. Alan Marlatt—one of the pioneers of American harm-reduction psychology and mindfulness-based craving control—and Jean Kristeller (1999) use the term "urge surfing," which is a gentler, yin-style metaphor. Our own smoking-cessation craving-control metaphor of smoking air is an attempt to strike a balance between yin and yang. Smoking, a behavior, connotes yang-style action. Smoking *air*, to our minds, connotes relaxing, yinlike breathing. As you flip the page, ponder which of these expressions feels more congruent with your mood. Smoke on it, if you need to.

Chapter 8

Training as If You Were on Fire

There is an expression in Zen: "Train as if your hair is on fire."
What does this mean? It means don't wait. Get immediately into
the present moment, and do what the moment requires.

—Cheri Huber, American Zen Teacher,
The Depression Book

A craving mind is a mind on fire. To survive the craving fires of the future,
you will have to train as if you were on fire *now*. After you quit smoking,
you will be bombarded by cravings to smoke. To survive this post-cessation
artillery, you will have to train as if you were under fire now. If chapter 6
was a recruiting station and chapter 7 was the armory, you are now on the
shooting range. What follows is advanced craving-control training. As
Taoist sage Lao-tzu once said: "To know and not to do is not yet to know."
Knowing about how to control cravings simply won't be enough. The task
at hand is to practice hijacking the smoking habit with a craving-control
habit. This might take you a couple of weeks, or it might take a couple of

months. How long it takes for you to climb this learning curve is entirely up to you. The good news is that you will have numerous daily opportunities to practice craving control while still smoking. So, there is no psychological downside whatsoever; you'll smoke to quit smoking. We will first introduce two levels of craving-control combat and then do a bit of target briefing.

Craving-Control Combat: Level 1

Craving-control combat is a kind of "smoking zazen." The Buddhist meditation-training known as *zazen* means "just sitting," literally and figuratively: literally in the sense of sitting through an urge, and figuratively as you endure the urge in a mentally settled manner. The specific goal of craving-control combat, level 1, is to *just sit* while your mind is ablaze with cravings and you have *an unlit cigarette* in your hand. Metaphorically speaking, the goal of this target practice is to set your mind on fire and to put it out with craving control. Your craving (desire, impulse) to smoke is the target. Your weapon of choice is smoking air (mindfulness-based, breath-focused craving control).

Here is the step-by-step training sequence:

1. Whenever you feel a craving to smoke, notice it and recognize the opportunity to practice craving control.

2. As you witness the craving, grab your cigarettes, go out to wherever you usually smoke, and sit down (if you can).

3. Get a cigarette ready, but do not light it; notice the craving intensify.

4. Smoke air to kill the initial craving (that is, engage in mindfulness-based, breath-focused meditation as you practiced in chapter 5).

5. After you've killed (defused) the initial craving, if the craving returns (that is, if you have another craving) and you feel like indulging this second craving, go ahead and smoke.

6. Mentally congratulate yourself on your craving-control success.

Level 1 Target Briefing

What constitutes a craving-control "kill"? That depends on the level of craving-control combat. Generally, a craving is a want, a state of desire; in this context, a desire to smoke. Cravings to smoke, like any desire, vary in intensity. A craving to smoke might take the form of a mild, fleeting thought, or it might present itself as a seemingly unstoppable urge. Cravings may also vary in duration and pattern. Thoughts and feelings of craving might zip through your mind like a flash flood or linger around, like a Christmas jingle, in a cyclical pattern. A successful craving-control "kill" doesn't mean that you made the craving go away for good. Not at all! Your level 1 objective is to survive this here-and-now craving. Whether or not you have a second craving is irrelevant at this point. Put differently, your training objective is to learn to survive one craving at a time. So, if you have a craving and witness it without acting on it until it subsides, that's a bona fide instant of craving-control success, even if the craving you killed is followed by another craving. To sum up, craving-control success is a fact of surviving a single, stand-alone craving without indulging it. A kill is a kill: it counts. A successful craving kill is when you watch the urge-related restlessness pass, when you survive the moment of the impulse without acting on it and return to your baseline of rational calmness.

Battle Stance: Sit Down

There is a Russian saying, *V nogakh pravdy nyet,* which means, "There is no truth in feet (in standing)," and there is a custom of starting every journey with a brief sit-down, *Syadyem na dorozhku!* which means, "Let's sit down before we hit the road" (Kaufman and Gettys 2006, 319). There is a good bit of old-world wisdom to this idea of claiming your time and not rushing the process. Just as a lot of smoking takes place on the go (while driving, pacing, or standing), much of modern-day smoking cessation, as we noted, is of the drive-through or quick-fix mentality. We invite you to change your smoking-cessation battle stance: sit down in craving-control zazen. As you practice craving control, literally sit down (whenever you can) to settle your mind.

Buddha Seat

Try the lotus sitting posture. Worry not; you don't have to change clothes and pretzel yourself into a full- or half-lotus position on a yoga mat. We have something far simpler than that in mind; we aren't talking about crossing your legs, we're talking about the palms-to-the-sun hand position atop your knees. This open-hand element is a powerful symbol of acceptance of whatever is. As you practice level 1 craving control, sit wherever you like (on the floor, a chair, your craving-control chair) with or without your legs crossed, with your palms up on top of your knees and an unlit cigarette in one of your hands, like a Buddha who was about to light up and got enlightened instead.

Craving-Control Oasis

All habits (healthy or unhealthy) thrive on cues. If you smoke at home, chances are you sit in the same spot to do it: in a favorite chair, on a porch swing, on a milk crate in the backyard, at the kitchen table. Hijack one of these smoking places! Pick a place where you've done a lot of smoking, and turn it into a craving-control oasis. Having a place like this can help you build a tradition of craving-control confidence, which will come in handy after you quit. When the urge to smoke strikes you at home, grab your cigarettes, go to your favorite smoking place, sit down with an unlit cigarette in your hands, and smoke air to get past the initial craving. After you kill the craving, if you still want to smoke, go to a different place in your home to smoke.

Craving-Control Combat: Level 2

You have the same target, your craving to smoke, and the same ammo, mindfulness-based and breath-focused craving control. But you have a different, more challenging training objective: whenever you feel like smoking, first candle-light a cigarette without taking the initial drag, just as you practiced in chapter 4; *while still holding the lit cigarette,* kill the initial craving; and then if you feel like it, smoke whatever remains of the cigarette. If you can sit down, do. If you can't, then stand, with your smoking hand pivoted forward, up, or both, letting your mind remain, in essence, on the "Buddha seat."

Here's the step-by-step level 2 training sequence:

1. Whenever you feel a craving to smoke, notice it and welcome the opportunity to practice craving control.

2. As you witness the craving, grab your cigarettes, go out to wherever you usually smoke, and sit down (if you can).

3. Candle-light a cigarette and notice your craving intensify.

4. Smoke air to kill the initial craving while the cigarette burns on.

5. After you've killed (defused) the initial craving, if the craving returns (that is, if you have a second craving) and you feel like indulging this second craving, go ahead and finish the cigarette.

6. Mentally congratulate yourself on your level 2 craving-control success.

Note: we do not recommend using level 2 craving control in your craving-control oasis. It would be counterproductive to associate any further smoking with this home-based craving-control fortress.

But Why? (Q&A)

We realize that these activities are pretty unorthodox. We anticipate that you have some questions at this point. Good, because we have some answers!

Why still smoke after you've killed the craving? This is a very important question, and it's essential that you are on the same page as we are about this. There are at least three good reasons to do this.

- **You are not yet ready to quit.** As you recall, we hypothesized earlier that the abysmal relapse rates are likely related to lack of craving-control readiness. So, it doesn't make good sense to quit smoking until you are skills ready. With this in mind, the question becomes, why *not* smoke? Indeed, if you are not yet skills ready to quit smoking, then why rush to quit prematurely? We suggest that you keep smoking until you are skills ready to quit, and use your smoking as the training ground for craving control.

- **You are gathering irrefutable, real-life success data.** The added benefit of this approach is that it allows you to create irrefutable success data proving that you can, in fact, control your cravings—right in the middle of the smoking scenario.

- **You are facilitating practice compliance.** Allowing yourself to smoke after you've killed the craving ensures that you will be motivated to kill the craving in the first place. Indeed, imagine that in the beginning of this craving-control training phase, you decide that if you succeed with defusing the real-life craving, you won't smoke afterward. So, you'd kill a few cravings and avoid a few cigarettes. Our prediction is that after a while, you'll start competing with yourself to do it every time, and in effect, you will slip into premature smoking cessation. All of a sudden, the optional craving-control practice will acquire the unnecessary self-imposed pressure of something mandatory. As a result, your focus will shift from honing your craving-control skills to making sure to avoid smoking. Put differently, you will get hung up on the outcomes of craving control rather than on learning the subtleties of its process.

But remember, you don't have to smoke after you kill the initial craving. It is entirely your choice. And making a mindful choice (of whether or not to smoke after you've killed the initial craving) is another essential element of your prep work for your ultimate goal of smoking cessation.

What if the craving returns? We expect the cravings to return. The goal is not to make all the cravings go away for good, but to practice surviving one craving at a time with the help of craving-control skillpower. As we see it, defusing the initial craving constitutes a precedent of craving-control success, even if you develop another craving and satisfy it by smoking afterward.

What if I want to kill the recurrent craving as well? You can. For example, you would kill the initial craving, and then if a second craving arises, you could decide to defuse it as well. If yet another craving arises, you might finally decide to indulge it by smoking. The point is to train as hard as you want; you can kill as many cravings per craving episode as you wish. That would be optimal but entirely unnecessary. In general, one craving-control kill per smoking episode is plenty of craving-control practice.

Will I need to practice craving control every time I want to smoke? That's entirely up to you. The goal is to get you skills ready. The more cravings you kill, the more skilled you are at craving control. For example, in the course of your day, you might have a craving to smoke after lunch and decide not to bother with craving control. That's fine. There'll be more craving-control practice opportunities throughout the day. The bottom line is that you don't have to kill every craving; you just have to eventually kill enough cravings to feel that you are in the ballpark of craving-control mastery.

On a related note, we strongly suggest that you allow yourself to just smoke now and then, without any kind of craving-control practice, while you are still in the training phase. Here's why: if you allow yourself to think of craving-control practice as something optional, then you are more likely to give it a try. If, however, you expect yourself to kill the craving every time you develop one, then this whole craving-control training business will begin to feel like a hassle. That's just human nature: we are far more likely to do something well if it's optional than if it's mandatory.

How much time should I spend on craving-control practice? No two smokers are alike. As important as quitting might be, chances are you have other, equally important priorities as well. We don't know you, so we won't even try to budget your time for you. Only you know what can and cannot wait in your life. The idea here is to get you skills ready. In other words, practice as long as it takes to get skills ready. How long will take? Days, weeks, months? Once again, we don't know, but here's what we suggest at a minimum:

1. Spend a month or so on mind work (chapter 4) and breath work (chapter 5).

2. Spend a few days on introductory craving-control training (chapter 7) to learn the nuts and bolts of the mindfulness-based, breath-focused craving-control technique, and then spend the rest of the month climbing the learning curve of real-life craving-control practice.

3. Spend at least a week on each level of craving-control training.

4. With several weeks of craving-control training under your belt, you'd be in a good place to test your craving-control skills readiness (chapter 14). If you pass the readiness test, then you are at a good place to plan your actual quit date. If you don't, that's useful feedback for you and an opportunity to fine-tune your craving-control skills.

Believe us, we understand that all this smoking-cessation business is a big hassle. We get it; you just want to be done with all this. And that is great. But we'd rather that you were overprepared than underprepared and felt you couldn't wait to quit than dreaded quitting. So, ultimately, the timeline is really up to you. You can fool around with craving-control training for, say, just a week and decide that you feel ready. And maybe you are! Who are we to know? If you feel you are ready, then test yourself to find out if your self-assessment matches reality. The bottom line is that it's your life and your timing. To offer you a rigid, one-size-fits-all timeline is to run the risk of rushing you to quit, and we have no desire whatsoever to repeat the mistakes of the drive-through smoking-cessation camp.

General Training Suggestions

There is no right or wrong way to do this. This training is just a blueprint. But here are some suggestions to help you get the most out of it.

Practice Level

Spend at least a week on each craving-control training level. The goal is to develop a sense of mastery. Once you go through both levels, decide whether you want to go ahead and test your skills readiness (chapter 14) or get some more craving-control practice under your belt. If you decide to continue with the practice, do so at the highest level possible to learn as much as you can. But, if you are having only intermittent success at level 2, then gear down to level 1 to reinforce the basics. If you are unable to pass the chapter 14 skills readiness test, we suggest starting over at level 1 and spending a week at each practice level as you review your craving-control basics. Accept the learning curve in advance!

Document Your Success

Whenever you successfully kill a craving, try to remember to draw a dot on the front or back of the cigarette pack as documentation. When you are done with the pack, cut out the front or back that has the craving-control dots, and save it. At some point add up all these craving-control kills to let the kill stats reassure you of your growing craving-control prowess.

Polish the Narrative

Practice your metaphor of choice, "killing the craving" or "surfing the craving wave," or simply keep reminding yourself to smoke air. So, when you develop a craving, hopefully your thought process will be a chain of reflexive self-instructions; for example:

Hmm, craving. Time to kill the craving. Nothing to do but smoke air. Notice the craving; exhale the craving. Good!

Hmm, craving. Big deal! Time to surf the waves. Notice the craving pass; refocus on your breath to exhale the craving. Good!

Hmm, craving. Back on the Buddha's seat to smoke air. Good!

Conclusion: Back to Your Original Nature

Any time you try to develop a habit, the new behavior feels awkward, unnatural. Once the habit takes root, it begins to feel like second nature. The goal is to make craving control a natural choice. The idea is to practice craving control to such a point of mastery that, in a manner of speaking, you return to your original nature, to that intuitive habit of thriving on unfiltered Mother-Nature air, to a baseline of just breathing and being. Smoking air, as the first-order response to your craving to smoke, is the way to get back to your breathing basics. Developing healthy habits, of course, takes time. So, claim your time. Continue smoking while practicing craving control, and keep reading (through part 4, on recovery-maintenance skills). Ready? Set. Take your time!

Part 4

Landing Gear: Recovery-Maintenance Skills

Before you start getting ready for the final approach, you will need to check your landing gear. By landing gear, in this context, we mean such recovery-maintenance skills as a platform of self-acceptance, lapse and relapse prevention training, and mindful eating (since post-cessation over-eating might sabotage your recovery goals). To ensure a safe landing, we will also test your craving-control skills readiness. We will also discuss the concept of the "smoke break" and offer you suggestions on how to translate your smoking habit into a platform of daily contemplative, breath-focused self-care. The goal is to complete your preparation for the final touchdown. We hope that by now, the ongoing doses of mindfulness have loosened your smoking so much that the habit no longer feels like habit and is beginning to feel like a hassle. In other words, if you feel that you can't wait to go ahead and quit, you are on the right track. Once you quit, life will be so much easier: you won't have to mess with any of this smoking-cessation prep work; instead, you'll move on with your life, dealing with occasional cravings on a per-need basis, calmly, dispassionately, and with unprecedented confidence. There's a lot to look forward to, and you are almost there!

Chapter 9

Platform of Choice Awareness

Smokers are conditioned to reach for a cigarette automatically.... A smoker can decrease the number of cigarettes smoked...with little conscious effort.

—Dr. Balasa Prasad, *Stop Smoking for Good*

Habits preempt choice: once a given behavior goes on autopilot, you just keep flying on a set course of habit. The goal of choice-awareness training is to leverage a greater baseline of choice awareness in your life. Being more aware of the choices available to you at any given point will be a great asset to you once you quit smoking. In the weeks after you have bought your last pack of cigarettes, much of your recovery will depend on whether you are on or off autopilot.

Rediscovering Freedom to Change

Mindlessness (automatic, habitual behavior) saves people time and energy. Habits are functional shortcuts that spare people the trouble of thinking and the hassle of conscious choice. The ability to learn a new behavior sequence and put it on autopilot is part of our amazing human efficiency, part of what helps us all excel. But, as powerful as habits are, they can also disempower you. It's exactly this mindlessness that makes habits hard to change. Habits are second nature in the sense that, just like other truly hardwired parts of your neuropsychology, they are hard to override. As such, habits disempower your freedom to change. This is why you experience a habitual behavior as *happening to* you rather than *being chosen by* you. Maybe you didn't consciously mean to light another cigarette, but you just found yourself with one in between your fingers. Like autopilot controlling a plane, habit flies by itself, unattended by its own mind. As such, a habit is a foreclosure on choice; functionally, mindlessness is choicelessness. A series of choice-awareness training exercises follows to help you spritz some mindfulness into the rusted gears of your automaticity.

The Circle of Choice

Induction: This prep exercise, taken from *Present Perfect* (Somov 2010b, 68), will help you develop a daily choice-awareness routine. Here are the instructions:

1. Take three sheets of paper and a pen.

2. Draw a circle on each sheet of paper, for a total of three circles.

Note: please, do not read any further until you have followed the previous steps.

Look at these circles. Chances are you have unintentionally drawn all three circles in more or less the same way. Indeed, we bet that the placement of the circles on each page is similar. We bet all three circles are somewhat similar in diameter. Most likely, they are similar in starting point (probably, between twelve o'clock and three o'clock). And, we bet all three circles were drawn in the same direction. Did you *consciously* intend for these circles to be similar in terms of page placement, size or diameter, direction, and starting point? Probably not.

In a sense, *you* did not draw these circles. The habit did! These circles, as evidenced by their unintentional similarities, have been drawn too mindlessly, too reflexively, too reactively, too mechanically, too robotically; that is, too unconsciously for you to take full, conscious credit for this action. This was a reaction—that is, a reenactment of some circle-drawing habit in your mind. True action involves conscious deliberation. Ponder this for a bit and realize that habits are just like these mindlessly drawn circles: mindless behavioral-feedback loops that flow in and out of themselves, the very stuff of the vicious cycles of the smoking habit that you got stuck in.

Intention: If habits are the wheels that keep people's lives spinning in circles, let's toss a monkey wrench into this cycle. We now invite you to draw another circle. But this time, draw a circle mindfully, with awareness of the options available to you. *Intend* the choices that you did not make the first time. *Choose* where on the page to place the circle, *choose* the starting point, *choose* the direction in which you will draw the circle, *choose* the diameter of the circle, and *choose* whether or not to bring the ends of the line together to complete the circle. Go ahead.

Integration: How was the experience of drawing this last circle different from the experience of drawing the first three circles? What are the different choices that you made? Or did you make the same choices as before but consciously this time? Did you draw this last circle, or did it just happen the way it did? Perhaps this time you felt that you were "actually" present. Congratulations, this time you *did* draw a circle.

Choice-Awareness Practice

Draw at least one mindful circle every day. Slow down enough to consciously take in all the options available to you at the moment: the hand you'll draw with, the placement of the drawing on the page, the starting point, the direction, the diameter, whether you will bring the ends of the line together or not. Use this exercise as an alarm clock for your mind.

Time this exercise strategically, before the events in your daily life that are fraught with compulsive mindlessness, such as smoking.

For the next week or so, when you are not practicing craving control, practice choice awareness. Right before you smoke, draw a mindful-choice circle right on the pack. Practice waking yourself up before you pop a cigarette in your mouth. Awaken the smoking zombie!

Broaden your choice-awareness practice. Go beyond smoking-related behavior. Think of this exercise as a kind of choice-awareness hygiene. Just as you brush your teeth every day (we presume), at some point or another, practice this circle-drawing exercise to leverage more mindfulness throughout your day.

Conclusion: Relax, You Have a Choice

Before you move on to the next chapter, try clenching your fist until your knuckles turn white. And now open it. White-knuckle it again, and open it again. White-knuckle it one more time, and open it one more time. Notice the pattern with which you open your hand. Now, white-knuckle your hand and open it with conscious awareness of the options available to you. You may start opening your hand with your thumb first or your little finger first, or you may open it in several brief bursts or with a rotation.

The point is that something as simple as opening your hand can open your mind. As a smoker, you've tried to white-knuckle it through your cravings before, trying to squeeze by on nothing but willpower. You don't have to white-knuckle through recovery anymore. Relax, you now have a choice. When, after quitting, you find yourself in the throes of a craving to smoke, trying to white-knuckle it because that's been your recovery autopilot so far, mindfully open your hand to both release the stress of the craving and to remind yourself of your craving-control options, to remind yourself to just smoke air.

Chapter 10

Platform of Self-Acceptance

Reports estimate that for nearly 70 percent of smokers, the possibility of failure stops them from trying to quit.... Don't let a fear of failure stop you from becoming a nonsmoker.

—American Cancer Society, *Kicking Butts*

Smokers dread quitting, not because they are terrified of post-cessation cravings. No, they fear an altogether different monster. They fear themselves, their own judgment, their own self-rejection, if they went back to smoking. You have nothing to fear. You always have been and always will be on your side, whether you smoke or not. Leveraging unconditional self-acceptance of this kind before quitting is essential to ensure a successful recovery.

Rethinking the Meaning of Mistakes

You always do your very best. Here's how we know it: reality never short-changes, and you are an inseparable part of this reality. There is no celestial layaway that saves up your potential to do better at any given point in time. You are manifesting fully, maxing out at any given point in time, as you continue climbing the learning curve of life, in general, and the learning curve of smoking cessation, in particular. It is essential that you understand this deep in your bones. When you do your best, which is all the time, there can be no mistakes, at least not in the conventional sense of the word. Here are a few exercises and discussions to help you understand what we mean by this provocative proclamation.

Make a Mistake; Fail on Purpose

The following exercise is taken from *Present Perfect* (Somov 2010b, 74). Fill a paper cup with water and drop it on the floor. Clean up the mess. Grab your house and car keys, and step outside your home. Go to your car and try to open it with your house key. Once you have done this unsuccessfully, go and try to open your house door with your car key. Once you've done this unsuccessfully, open the door with the correct key, go inside, and return to reading. Congratulate yourself for successfully completing this exercise. Ask yourself *Is a mistake made on purpose a mistake?* Smoke on it, mindfully, if you have to. Conclude that a *chosen* behavior is not a mistake; a mistake that is made (as in a *consciously* chosen or selected course of action) is not a mistake.

No One Makes Mistakes on Purpose

The phrase "to make a mistake" implies action initiated on purpose, doesn't it? But that's fundamentally inaccurate: there are no intentional mistakes; no one consciously sets out to fail. And when you fail on purpose, when you make a mistake by design, you actually succeed. Think about the exercise you just did: in trying to fail on purpose, you succeeded. The task was to fail, and you did fail. When you consciously set out to make a mistake, you are trying to successfully carry out a subversive intention. An act of conscious sabotage isn't a mistake (to you) even if it takes the form of a mistake (to others). How is this relevant to smoking cessation and all this quitting business? No one lapses or relapses on purpose. Sure, after a period of abstinence from your drug of choice, you might choose to use again, but that's not because you want to lapse or relapse. No, it's because at a moment like that—probably due to inordinate stress, lack of skillpower, or both—you decide to use a form of chemical coping. Such a moment is not a mistake, but an instant of self-medication—that is, a moment of self-care. Sure, in hindsight, you might think *I could've done better; I didn't have to use* (smoke, drink, and so on). *I could've used craving control.* The reality is that you could not have; if you could have, you would have. History isn't optional. History is not a story of theoretical possibilities, but a story of facts, a narrative of real-life necessities. So, to look back at a past moment of chemical self-care and conclude that you "made" a mistake, to think that you relapsed "on purpose," to conclude that your moment of chemical coping was an act of self-sabotage, now that would be a mistake of self-rejection! We'll come back to this in a moment. In the meantime, recognize that no one *makes* mistakes, yet mistakes do take place.

Drop the Ball

Life is a series of variables, and surviving is a juggling act. Now and then, we *all* drop the proverbial ball, not because we intend to, but because there are too many balls to juggle. Understanding the difference between an intentional mistake and an unintentional occurrence is key. With this in mind, try juggling (Somov 2010b, 75). Fruits with rinds are best (oranges, limes, lemons) because they won't burst when dropped. First, drop the "ball" on purpose. That's failure on demand. Now, try to juggle until you drop it by accident. Alternate between failure-on-demand mode and juggle-until-failure mode. It's essential that you see the difference. Chances are your life is already busy and complex. And now you've added yet another variable to this equation of living, this project of quitting smoking. Recognize that you have no intention whatsoever to shortchange yourself. Recognize that you will do your practical, not theoretical, best. Recognize that, whatever the outcome, your best is enough.

A Mistake Isn't Evidence of Self-Sabotage

To sum up, a mistake isn't evidence of self-sabotage. Say you rush through the process and quit too soon, before you feel skills ready and then, before too long, find yourself once again with a cigarette in your mouth. Does that mean that you have intentionally sabotaged your efforts to quit? Of course not! You'll do your best, but your best might not be enough. That's the way it is with complex undertakings. Quitting smoking is hard, because smoking is such a profoundly ingrained habit. So, if you quit on an impulse, you just might end up with a whopper of a craving, and after doing your best at white-knuckling, you still might get overwhelmed by the intensity of the urge and light up. Whether you manage to wing it or not, whether you stay abstinent or not, one thing is clear to us: you will do your best. You might say, "Hold it, buddy! If I rushed to quit too soon, then how could I still assert that I did my best?" So what if you rushed? So, you overestimated your skills readiness; that makes a certain sense. On some level, this kind of premature cessation is existentially self-affirming. You overbanked on willpower: you decided to wing it once more; that's confidence. So, you already have confidence; that's good! Now, let's cultivate self-acceptance and get back to craving-control school to double up on skillpower. Live and learn! The bottom line is that you always do your practical, here-and-now best. What's left is for you to get this idea into your bones. The following discussion and several exercises will help you internalize the idea that *you always do your best.*

Making Sense of Your Past Efforts to Quit

Your past efforts to quit say nothing about your future. When you quit before, you didn't know what you know now. You didn't train as if you were on fire. You either tried to wing it on a patch and a prayer, or you were prematurely rushed into recovery through some kind of misguided drive-through smoking-cessation program. But if you feel like digging for lessons in your past, the next couple of exercises are for you.

Looking for "Your Best" In Unlikely Places

When people think of their "bests," the instances in which they fully maxed out and gave it all they could, they tend to think of their big-time accomplishments and moments of glory. But, as we see it, even mistakes and failures are evidence of people's best efforts. Analyze your last two or three smoking-cessation attempts to find your "best" in them. Let us give you an example of a classic dialogue that comes up in smoking-cessation therapy as we take a look at past mistakes concerning quitting. Say you quit and stayed quit for a couple of weeks but then went back to smoking.

Therapist. So, last time you tried to quit, you stayed abstinent for almost two months but then lapsed? How do you think this happened?

Smoker. I decided to test myself to see if I could smoke one and walk away.

Therapist. Was it wrong of you to test yourself?

Smoker. No, not wrong, just unnecessary. Life's full of challenges and tests, and I was passing those tests just fine until I decided to test myself on purpose. I should not have done that!

Therapist. Then why did you do that?

Smoker. I thought I could; I was just trying to prove something to myself.

Therapist. Was it wrong to think that you could pass a test? Was it wrong to feel confident?

Smoker. I guess not, but if I hadn't been thinking like that, I'd still be smoke free.

Therapist. Did you know that you would go back to smoking as a result of that test?

Smoker. Of course not! Otherwise it wouldn't have been a test. Not at all. When I tested myself, I felt pretty good about my ability to stay away from the smokes, so I just thought I'd test myself to end the internal debate.

Therapist. What debate?

Smoker. I had wondered if I could just smoke now and then, you know, recreationally, so I decided to test myself.

Therapist. So, you didn't realize that with these thoughts, you were not merely wondering, but entertaining a form of craving?

Smoker. I guess I didn't; I wasn't thinking of things in those terms then. Now that I understand how cravings work and what to do about them, I'd just kill the craving and move on. I didn't know then that I could test my craving control before I quit as part of the craving-control training. I just quit, as before, on an impulse, without any skills, really. I guess, given what little I knew about all this craving-control stuff, I did *my best*. The fact is, in retrospect, I am surprised at how well I did.

This dialogue is, of course, tuned up a bit, but the gist of it is pretty classic: when somebody starts grilling you on the specifics of why you did or didn't do something, you tend to come to your own defense and eventually realize that, even though your course of action led to an undesirable outcome, you didn't really mean to screw up or inconvenience anyone. You realize that you did your best. So, before you read on, go down memory lane and analyze your recent smoking-cessation mistakes to find your "best" in them.

Shoulda, Coulda, Woulda, Buddha

When people make a mistake, they tend to beat themselves up. This self-loathing habit is an obstacle to recovery. So, before you formally begin to quit, take the time right now to practice turning rumination into acceptance. Upgrade your self-rejecting "shoulda, coulda, woulda" mantra by substituting "buddha" (Somov 2010b, 78). *Buddha* means "awakened, enlightened" in Pali. Use this term in its lowercase connotation as a symbol of acceptance and appreciation of the *ordinary perfection* of what is. What do we mean by "ordinary perfection"? Simply, this life, right now; whatever it is right now is all there is. So, when you find yourself ruminating on some recent mistake or imperfection, toss a little "buddha" into your self-talk. Recognize that whatever you did, you did your best, and even if that was not enough for others, it is enough for you. What else could you have done, be better than you were at that moment in time? Wake up to the impossibility of that! "Shoulda, coulda, woulda, buddha." You were what you were. You are what you are. You will be what you will be, never less than you are, never more than you are—just you, doing your practical (not theoretical) best. What's not to accept?

Conclusion: Acceptance-Based Recovery

Chances are when you dropped the ball in the "Drop the Ball" exercise, you didn't criticize yourself (unless you happen to be a professional juggler). You probably attributed your inability to keep the balls in the air to the complexity of the task. In other words, you accepted the learning curve. Recognize that quitting smoking is a difficult thing to do. So, accept the learning curve ahead of you in order to accept yourself, and accept yourself in order to accept the learning curve ahead of you. Realize that you are not at risk for self-sabotage. You are on your own side. You are not going to make a mistake on purpose. If you lapse (smoke just one cigarette) or relapse (smoke a whole pack or go back to smoking altogether), it's not because some invisible demon inside you tripped you up. No, it'll be because going back to smoking, which is just a form of chemical coping, will be your best coping effort for dealing with the *stress of smoking cessation*. Face it: quitting smoking is stressful; that's why it's essential that you lighten up on yourself a bit. If you quit and then lapse or relapse, if that's how it plays out, then so be it; you don't have to beat yourself up for trying. Just reshuffle the deck of smoking cessation at that point and deal yourself a new hand of cards. So, as you look ahead, give yourself a break: accept, in advance, on a wholesale level, unconditionally, that any outcome of your smoking-cessation endeavors will be evidence of your doing the best you can. Take your time in building this platform of self-acceptance; it's a vital part of your smoking-cessation prep work. Don't just zip through this section; mull it over, think it through, and smoke on it—mindfully—if you need to. Dare to rethink the meaning of "mistake" to eliminate the possibility of failure!

Chapter 11

Broadening the Margin of Error

Relapse should be regarded as part of the learning
experience along the pathway to cessation.

—David Abrams and Raymond Niaura,
The Tobacco Dependence Treatment Handbook

Relapse prevention (that is, having a plan for how to get back on track
should you lapse or relapse) is an old clinical staple in addiction literature.
Relapse-prevention literature is essentially self-acceptance literature. In our
view, however, relapse-prevention literature tends to underestimate the
fundamental conflict between the typical puritanical Western psyche and
the self-acceptance in relapse prevention. The Western mind is pretty hard
on itself and tends to take a catastrophic view of any deviation from the
original plan, turning it into a self-esteem crisis—which is why we first offer
to cultivate the platform of self-acceptance. Now that you have had a
chance to reacquaint yourself with yourself, now that you have hopefully
had a chance to recognize that you are your best ally, not your worst enemy,

you are in a position to build a viable relapse-prevention plan on this foundation. A relapse-prevention plan without a foundation of self-acceptance is a castle in the sky, just another clinical puff of smoke, more of a tantalizing promise of a plan than a psychologically actionable plan. In sum, chapter 10 was an attempt to get your recovery perfectionism out of the way in order to make room for relapse-prevention training. So here we go.

Make Room for the Learning Curve

In *Fast Facts: Smoking Cessation*, Robert West and Saul Shiffman (2007, 49), in discussing relapse, report that research shows "that [former] smokers who smoke at all, even a puff, are almost certain to relapse." This is an incredibly small margin of error, isn't it? Actually, is it even a margin of error at all if a single puff is tantamount to a conclusion of failure? The goal of this chapter is to broaden the margin of error with the help of slip, lapse, and relapse prevention training. This chapter, of course, is designed to work in unison with the chapter on self-acceptance. Our hope is that you have definitively established that you always do the best that you can, not some theoretical best but your practical best. So, while you stand on this firm ground of self-acceptance, you need to, just in case, lay out a cushion should you fall once or twice.

Slip, Lapse, Relapse

The goal of slip, lapse, and relapse prevention training is to help you stay abstinent from smoking—that is, to prevent abstinence loss. In our analysis, there is substantial confusion about what constitutes loss of abstinence. If your dermatologist (skin doctor), without any testing, told you that a dark spot on your forearm was melanoma and turned out to be wrong, you'd never go to that doctor again. The recovery industry does this sort of thing every day when it confuses a slip with a lapse and a lapse with a relapse. These three are, of course, not the same. So, let's, once and for all, end this lingering confusion and make sense of abstinence loss with the help of a "banana peel" metaphor that we developed for working with substance users.

Slip and Slip Prevention

Say you are walking down the street and see a banana peel. When you see the banana peel and realize its slippery potential, you might walk around it to avoid a slip. In this see-but-not-slip scenario, you are preventing a slip (slip prevention). If you hadn't been paying attention, you would have stepped on the banana peel and slipped—that is, lost your balance.

What's the banana peel in this scenario? The banana peel here is a metaphor for a craving. A craving, as you recall, is when you are living your life in a state of functional balance, and then, bam—you want something really badly, and your mind starts leaning toward something that you want, almost tipping and falling over unless you catch it with craving control. So, in this case, a smoking-cessation slip is when you have a desire to smoke after you quit. How can you prevent a slip? By staying away from whatever it is that triggers your smoking. For example, if you quit yesterday and have dinner in the smoking section of a restaurant today out of habit, you are dancing on the banana peel of craving. But even though you have not prevented the emergence of the craving, even though your craving mind jeopardizes your recovery balance, it doesn't mean that it is too late and you will fall. Of course it's not too late. You can still prevent a lapse. Read on.

Lapse and Lapse Prevention

Say you are walking down the street without paying attention. So, you step on a banana peel and, as a result, slip up; that is, you lose your balance. Reflexively, you flail your arms and gyrate your torso to regain your balance. And voilà! You do not fall, despite having slipped. You regain your balance and prevent a fall. In this slip-without-falling scenario, you prevent a lapse (a fall), which constitutes lapse prevention. Distinguishing between a slip and a lapse makes good sense. An act of slipping does not equal an act of falling; the two are psychologically and behaviorally different events, which is reflected in the actual semantics of the words involved: a "lapse" literally means a fall; a "slip" does not mean a fall and therefore does not equal a lapse.

Let's pick up the craving scenario that we put on hold a moment ago. You quit yesterday; today, out of mindless habit—which is natural—you find yourself eating in the smoking section of a restaurant, feeling overwhelmed by a craving. The fact is it's too late to prevent a slip—that is, to prevent the craving; you are already tap-dancing on a banana peel, compliments of mindlessness. But just because you are losing balance doesn't mean you have to fall—that is, lapse. No, you can still prevent a lapse. How? With craving control. Kill the craving to regain your balance.

Relapse and Relapse Prevention

Say you are walking down the street without paying attention. You step on the banana peel and slip—that is, lose your balance. You flail your arms and gyrate your torso to no avail. You are not able to regain your balance, so you fall (lapse). As you try to get back on your feet, you might fall again (relapse). The three reasons you might fall again while trying to get back up are (1) you got too hurt and it is too painful to get back up; (2) you lose your balance and fall again as you try to get up; and (3) you feel a little shaky and unsteady on your feet, and because you have nothing to lean on or support yourself with, you fall back down. If, however, you look around and mindfully size up what you need in order to safely get back on your feet, if perhaps you first calm down, rest, and ask for help to get back on your feet, you just might be able to prevent another fall (relapse), which would constitute relapse prevention.

Let's get back to our restaurant scenario. You quit yesterday and mindlessly found yourself in the smoking section of your neighborhood restaurant, feeling overwhelmed by a craving to smoke. Is it too late to prevent a slip (a craving)? Yes, you already have a whopper of a craving and can't go back in time to a moment before you chose where to sit. So, slip prevention is out of the question. What are you trying to do? You are trying to regain your mind's balance. How? By using craving control. So, here you are: having slipped on the banana peel of craving, you are trying to regain balance with the help of craving control. But, let's say you can't. Even though you are doing your best, the craving gets the best of you. So, you bum a cigarette, smoke it, and return to finish your meal. What happened here? You lapsed. First, you slipped—that is, got a craving. Then, you tried to prevent the fall, the lapse, with the help of craving control, and it didn't work. So, you lapsed; you had one cigarette. What's next to prevent a relapse? What would be a relapse in this situation? The relapse here would be to decide that you are done with this smoking-cessation effort, at least done for now, and to buy a pack on the way back home. Now, just because you have lapsed, or fallen, doesn't mean you have to stay down. You can still prevent a relapse. How? With the same old craving control and access of support if you need to. (We'll discuss the issue of accessing support later.)

Premature Quitting of Quitting

Here's what we want to help you prevent with our approach. First, we'd like to help you prevent a premature decision to quit smoking. We've been massaging this point from the beginning: if you are only motivationally ready, you aren't ready to quit. Put differently, if you are not skills ready to quit smoking, you are not ready to quit. We hope that's clear. Second, with this discussion we are trying to help you prevent premature quitting of the actual quitting process once you have initiated it. Let us clarify: say you quit yesterday, and today you lapsed. If you confuse a slip with a lapse or a lapse with a relapse, you'll prematurely quit the quitting process.

We've seen this happen time and again. Quite a few substance-use clients have told us that once they had quit their substance of choice and stumbled onto a whopper of a craving, they started second-guessing themselves and quit the quitting process—that is, went from a slip to a full-blown relapse, from a craving back to using. Their thinking was *If I want to use that badly, then I must not want to quit.* This is a classic missed lapse-prevention opportunity. People find themselves having a craving (which is to be expected) and misinterpret the craving as a loss of commitment to abstinence. So, instead of using craving control to steady the unbalanced mind, they bypass lapse prevention and dive headfirst back into their typical using patterns, going from a trivial slip to a full-blown relapse. Alternatively, a person lapses—for example, uses once—and prematurely concludes: *I used once, so I am done.* No, you are not; just because you could not control a craving and used once (lapsed) doesn't mean that you have to go back to full-blown using (smoking, drinking, and so on). Having lapsed, you can still prevent a relapse. Quitting the process of quitting after a lapse, let alone a slip, is premature. This discussion is to help you avoid this foreclosure.

Knowing the differences among slip, lapse, and relapse isn't enough. You also have to have solid craving-control skills (which you are still working on) and compassion for your recovery efforts (which you are also working to leverage). You've done the best that you could throughout your slips, lapses, or relapses. And you will continue to do the best that you can, whether you slip, lapse, or relapse. Recovery isn't simple, so help yourself by opening up your recovery options. Give yourself permission to continue with the quitting process even if you slip, even if you lapse, and even if you relapse. Give yourself this permission now, not later. Put the book aside and think: *I'll be at it until I get it done. A slip won't stop me. A lapse won't stop me. A relapse won't stop me. I've got the rest of my life to lick this habit!*

Peel a Few Bananas

Now, we are not suggesting that you set yourself up for a slip, lapse, or relapse. You wouldn't consciously make that mistake anyway. By suggesting that you "peel a few bananas," we are playfully suggesting that you do some retrospective analysis of your past smoking-cessation efforts. Analyze what happened in terms of the banana peels of your temptations. Think of the last time you quit the quitting process, and ask yourself *Did I slip on the banana peel of craving, and because I didn't know what to do about the craving, lapse? And not yet knowing that a lapse isn't the same as a relapse, did I just prematurely quit the quitting process?* Review several such instances to make sense of the missed prevention opportunities.

Practice this thought process. It'll come in handy after you buy your last pack of cigarettes. Also, take a moment to imagine yourself in a variety of situations in the future, thinking through them using the banana-peel metaphor. For example, imagine yourself having a craving and analyzing it as follows: *Okay, what's going on here in terms of the banana peel metaphor? I am slipping up by having a craving and losing my mind's balance. What do I need to do metaphorically? I need to catch my balance to prevent a fall, a lapse. Just because I have slipped on a banana peel doesn't mean I have to fall. How can I keep myself from falling? I need to kill this craving to restore my mind's balance.* Or, imagine yourself having lapsed, having smoked one cigarette. Take yourself through the following process: *Okay, I smoked a cigarette. What does that mean in terms of the banana-peel metaphor? I lapsed. But a lapse isn't a relapse. Just because I slipped, stumbled, and fell doesn't mean that I have to stay down. Not all is lost yet. The fact is nothing's lost. I knew it might be part of this process, part of this learning curve. So, what do I do now? I need to prevent a relapse. How? By continuing to kill any further cravings and, if need be, accessing some social support.*

Conclusion: A Prevention Plan Isn't Permission to Smoke

In our work with substance-use clients, the idea of preparing for what to do if you slip, lapse, or relapse is sometimes seen as permission to do so. Let's see if this idea holds water. If you had a choice between two identical cars priced the same, one with air bags and one without, which would you take? The one with the air bags, we presume. Does that mean that just because you have a protection plan in the event of a collision, you will now allow yourself to wreck the car anytime you want? Of course not! It's the same with slip, lapse, or relapse prevention planning: having a good prevention plan is no different from having air bags. Giving yourself permission to continue quitting, despite a slip or lapse, is not self-destructive, but self-preserving. But for now, ponder your fear of having a lapse and relapse prevention plan. Mindfully smoke on it, if you need to, while you still smoke.

Chapter 12

Platform of Dosed Self-Care

Our grand business is not to see what lies dimly at a
distance, but to do what lies clearly at hand.

—Thomas Carlyle

Smoking is coping. But it's not just coping; it's also a form of dosed or paced coping. We briefly alluded to this in chapter 1, if you recall. Unlike most nonsmokers, who get stressed and stressed and stressed until they sit down for a moment of self-care (if they remember to do that at all!), you've been coping as you go, asserting your well-being through a series of timed mini (smoking) breaks. Thanks to your smoking, you have developed an excellent meditative platform of taking time for yourself on a per-need basis. Indeed, whenever you have felt like smoking, you've temporarily retired from the hustle and bustle of your daily grind for a contemplative smoke break.

It is essential that you keep this daily *infrastructure of self-care*. The problem all these years hasn't been the fact that you've stepped out for a "breather," but that you've breathed junky, tobacco-poisoned air. The goal of this book is to help you kick tobacco, *not* this amazing habit of breath-focused, contemplative, dosed self-care. So, as you inch toward smoking cessation, let's take a detailed look at this platform of dosed self-care that you have built, to avoid tossing your self-care baby out with the bathwater of tobacco.

Ample Self-Care

Smoking, as strange as it sounds, is a form of active, if not proactive, coping. You feel stress building up and decide to take a smoke break. That's assertive self-care. But here's what tends to happen when you quit smoking: you notice stress building up, and you do nothing. That's a loss of self-care time. When you add up all these missed mini breaks, that's a lot of self-care time lost. Let's do some simple math here. Say it takes you a total of five minutes from when you decide to go out for a smoke to when you come back from a smoke. If you are a pack-a-day smoker, that's about an hour and a half's worth of your time per day. That's a hell of a lot of self-care time to throw away along with tobacco. Before, when you tried to quit smoking, you also inadvertently quit all this invaluable self-care time! No wonder you eventually relapsed: not only did you have to mourn the loss of a smoking habit, but you also deprived yourself of a very substantial chunk of self-care time.

Keep the Smoke Break

We emphatically suggest that you keep the smoke break after you quit smoking; just make it smoke free. In other words, keep the infrastructure of your self-care intact. Doing so is pivotal. More specifically, we recommend that in the first month after you finally quit smoking, you take exactly as much self-care time as you had previously spent on smoking. Now, some of this time will be spent smoking air. But even if you don't have any cravings or they subside as you go along, we highly recommend that you continue to take self-care breaks (formerly smoke breaks) with roughly the same regularity as you did when you smoked.

Calculate Your Smoke-Break Time

While you are still actively smoking is the time to calculate how much time you actually spend on your daily smoking routine. Use your watch to time the duration of an average smoke break, and multiply it by the average number of cigarettes you smoke. Calculate the total amount of time. Both numbers, the total time and the average smoke-break time, are important data. After you quit for good, it'll be important to know what your total daily self-care time budget is and how to break it up into rest breaks. If you are in the habit of chain-smoking and usually don't take actual smoke breaks, then we suggest you start to do so while you are still smoking. As you settle in to this temporary routine of taking smoke breaks, calculate the total daily self-care time.

Making Good Use of Your Smoke-Free Smoke Break

What shall you do during these breaks? Smoke air (to prevent any possible cravings and to relax). And then rest in whatever manner pleases you, read a few pages of a book, work on a crossword, check your personal e-mails, or fool around on the Internet. The point is that you hold on to your self-care time, no matter what, with the same creative stubbornness that previously allowed you to squeeze regular smoking into the nooks and crevices of any given day of your life.

Review Your Smoke-Break Patterns and Devise Alternatives

To ensure a smooth transition to your post-tobacco life, it would be useful to re-create your self-care routine to the extent possible. Here's what we mean. Let's say that during workdays, you do most, if not all, of your smoking outside. It would be a good idea, post-cessation, to take your smoke-free breaks mostly outside as well. To facilitate that, you will have to come up with some creative alternatives. During your smoking work life, you probably smoked outside in a designated smoking area, but you would be well advised to avoid it after quitting smoking. So, to successfully re-create your self-care routine, you'll have to go on a couple of scouting missions to see what your new outside options are. This way, after you quit smoking, you can still take your smoke-free breaks outside, but instead of spending them in the smoking-trigger zones, you will perhaps go for a brisk walk around the corner, sit on a nearby bench, or just lean on a wall and gaze at a tree, while smoking air, either for craving control or the sheer pleasure of it. So, while you still smoke, we invite you to review the "topography" of your current smoke breaks. Explore the usual context in which you take this time for yourself, and begin to envision how you can hold on to this context in a smoke-free manner after you have finally quit.

Keep the Crew

As we noted initially, smoking, particularly in this day and age of social harassment of smokers, can be a powerful bonding context. Smokers huddle together, come rain or snow, in these pitiful designated smoking areas, like brooding penguins. Shared stigma and proximity make for solid social connections. Our recommendation is that you keep your comrades in arms. Now, we are not saying that you should try to hook up with them with the same regularity that you did in your smoking days. That's bound to produce unnecessary cravings. What we are suggesting is that you let them know you have quit but that you haven't quit them, particularly in the event that you have formed a more-than-superficial social connection with somebody. The point is kick the tobacco, but keep the relationships you have worked to form, particularly if they are meaningful to you. They might not be; you might discover that once the smoking is gone, so is the rapport. But you might also realize that the connections you have built can withstand the loss of smoking as a common denominator. You might realize that what started out as a smoking connection has long evolved into a quality acquaintance, if not friendship. We suggest you keep that. How?

Consider cultivating other opportunities for hooking up. If you have a lunchtime smoking partner, invite that person for a walk around the parking lot instead. Or, if the connection feels worth preserving, consider some other shared social engagements. But if push comes to shove and the only way you can touch base with so-and-so is during the person's cigarette break, then you just might have to join in—by smoking air. Chances are your friend will be duly impressed by your ability to hang out together for a few minutes without lighting up. After your friend sees you do that a few times, the person might just pick your brain for smoking-cessation know-how.

Now, we are not suggesting that you unnecessarily test yourself in this way. There is no need for any contrived testing. Life is plenty full of tests and curveballs. What we are suggesting is that you weigh your options and know that, if need be, you don't have to lose a friendship over a cigarette, particularly when you have some tried-and-true craving-control power tools under your belt.

Five Self-Care Tips

Here are five self-care tips that will come in handy:

- If you do not make a conscious effort to take frequent but brief smoke-free smoke breaks (self-care breaks) throughout the day, you will handicap your recovery. We encourage you to keep the infrastructure of dosed self-care that you have risked your health to develop throughout the years. Collect the dividends of your chemical coping investments.

- As a nicotine-dependent smoker, you take smoke breaks because your body compels you to. If you don't, the body begins to blackmail you with withdrawal symptoms. After you quit smoking and work your way through withdrawal, the inner whip of physiological dependence is no longer there, and it's all too easy to postpone these self-care breaks you have come to rely on. Don't. Whatever you feel you need to focus on, the far more important business is to take care of yourself in a time of need. If you feel stressed and think you cannot afford to take a few minutes for yourself, your judgment is, indeed, affected by stress. Recognize that a mind in a rush is not to be trusted. Your self-care time is not a frivolity but a basic responsibility of living.

- Instead of counting how long you've been "clean" and relying on time as some kind of recovery crutch, use time as a tool. Take time for yourself, just as you do when you smoke, and this self-care time will eventually add up to "clean time" on its own.

- As a smoker, your journey of self-care is a well-trodden path. Once it's time to smoke, you go on an all-too-familiar trip (of relocating to a smoking area, lighting up, perhaps even connecting with a smoking sojourner). After you quit, you'll have to reinvent the itinerary a bit. But the journey doesn't have to be anything all that fancy; you don't have to go to India. Just take a few minutes several times throughout the day to close your eyes and trip on smoking air.

- An unknown Yoga master once said, "Your breathing is your greatest friend. Return to it in all your troubles, and you will find comfort and guidance." After you quit, smoke air ten to twenty times a day for as long as it now takes for you to smoke a cigarette. Whether or not you have a craving to smoke, take your smoke-free smoke break to ensure the long-term success of your recovery.

Conclusion: Keep the Habit of Self-Care

To reiterate, keep the platform of self-care breaks—that is, the regimen of brief, contemplative, breath-focused breaks. To help you remember this, as of now, begin to think of your smoking, while you are still in the training or prep phase, as self-care time. Instead of telling yourself or others that it's time for a smoke, think or announce that it's time for self-care. From this point on, think of any leftover smoking as "you" time, as break time. Remember that your smoking life has been, in essence, a life of breath-focused contemplation. Remember to keep this habit as you kick the tobacco. Treasure these solitary, quiet moments with yourself. You've paid with your body for this meditative habit of slowing down during the rat race of modern living. You deserve to keep what you have built one breath at a time. In sum, the goal is to shift from smoke breaks to smoke-free breaks, without losing the backbone of your self-care. You will need it to support your recovery efforts.

Chapter 13

Mindful Oral Coping

Dieting while quitting is not helpful.... [D]ietary restriction
can lead to feelings of deprivation, which in turn can
precipitate either inappropriate eating...or smoking in an
effort to cope with the perceived deprivation.

—Kenneth Perkins, Cynthia Conklin, and
Michele Levine, *Cognitive-Behavioral
Therapy for Smoking Cessation*

Both smoking and emotional eating are forms of *oral coping*. Both involve
putting something in your mouth. Both of these behaviors are pacifiers of
the mind. There is a chance that after you have quit one oral habit, that
of smoking, the other oral-coping behavior, that of emotional eating (such
as eating to cope with boredom, anxiety, or stress), will kick into gear. In
the overall scheme of things, this kind of coping substitution isn't a big
deal. Indeed, if it takes a minor, short-term weight gain to kick the tobacco
habit, then so be it. You'll have the rest of your life to get your weight
under control once you have stopped smoking. But if you are going to eat
to cope (eat emotionally), you might as well do it mindfully. That's right:
emotional eating isn't the problem; it's the *mindless* emotional *overeating*

that is the problem. A mindfully enjoyed cookie instead of a cigarette won't kill you and might help you get by during the initial post-cessation period. Thus, the goal of this chapter is to equip you with a bit of mindful eating know-how before you quit smoking so that you can use mindful eating, in general, to check your post-cessation runaway appetite and mindful emotional eating, in particular, as a backup oral-coping choice.

Going off the Tobacco Diet

Smoke is calorie free, and this hasn't escaped the attention of the ever weight-obsessed West. Smoking has been and remains one of the most popular "diets." As a stimulant, nicotine suppresses appetite. If weight is a concern for you and if you have managed your weight with smoking, then now is exactly the time to begin the transition from "tobacco diet" to mindfulness-based management of overeating. Furthermore, cultivating mindful-eating skills will facilitate your smoking-cessation prep work. You see, much of mindful eating know-how is highly compatible with the awareness-building, habit-modifying, and craving-control prep work that is part of this smoking-cessation program.

From Chain Eating to Mindful Eating

Mindless grazing is just like chain-smoking. Eating, like smoking, is a complex motor behavior that consists of the coordination of arms, hands, neck, and mouth. Tossing a monkey wrench into the eating movements does wonders to awaken the eating zombie. The following are a few pattern-interrupting exercises to help you infuse your eating moments with more presence.

Right Food, Wrong Hand

Try eating with your nondominant hand. Note how this confuses your mind and increases your mindfulness.

Right Food, Wrong Utensil

Utensils are part of the hypnotic ritual of eating. They cue your hands (and minds) to a certain sequence of motor behaviors. That's the utility of a utensil. Let's make utensils useless, in order to make more use of the mind. Try eating with wrong utensils. Use chopsticks instead of a fork (if you are not used to eating with chopsticks). Use a spoon instead of a fork (with, say, green beans). Switch things up. Even try eating with your hands instead of utensils. Notice your mind wake up as it is forced to make new choices.

Old Mouth, New Food

Awaken your mind with new food. After you quit smoking, your taste and smell will come back online. Your mouth will feel new. All of a sudden you might develop extra curiosity about the flavor of food. To keep that curiosity from becoming a runaway appetite, practice flavor awareness. Try new foods. Having interesting snacks around will help you rein in any mindless post–smoking-cessation snacking by refocusing on the quality of the experience, instead of the quantity of the food.

Control the Munchies to Help Yourself Quit Smoking

A craving is a craving is a craving. Practice food-related craving control to prevent overeating after you have quit smoking. Remember that by now, with all the smoking-related craving-control training you've done, you are pretty well defended. So, you don't have to fear your favorite foods. What follows is exposure-based craving-control combat—for the munchies.

Brave the Munchies: Level 1

Purchase one of your favorite foods. Bring it home and let it sit in view. Allow a craving to emerge. For level 1 practice, first defuse the craving (with the help of mindfulness-based, breath-focused witnessing), and then if you feel like it, indulge. Congratulate yourself on your craving-control success. Practice this kind of craving control in parallel with your other quit-date preparations.

Brave the Munchies: Level 2

Procure something else that tends to call out your name from the fridge or pantry. When you hear the call of the craving, set your mind on craving fire: taunt yourself with one bite. Notice the craving for more, set the food aside, and defuse the cravings until you feel that you can easily walk away from the food in front of you. When you get to this point, congratulate yourself on your craving-control success. If, at this point or soon after, you feel like finishing the treat, have a couple of *mindful* bites. Enjoy! Repeat this type of munchies control in parallel with the rest of your quit-date preparations.

Mindful Substitutions

In your previous attempts at quitting, you might have tried to stock up on candy, or chew toothpicks, plastic straws, or flavored gum. Here are a couple of exercises to help you tune up your repertoire of substitutions.

A Drag of Mint?

While the term "finish" is known as a measure of wine, few apply it to food. The finish is both an aftertaste and an after feel (a residual feel in the mouth). As a smoker, you are not new to this concept. Various brands of tobacco have different kinds of mouth feel. Practice noticing the mouth feel of the foods you eat. If you have been smoking flavored tobacco, this is a particularly important exercise. Identify foods with the mouth feel that is vaguely similar to the mouth feel and taste of the tobacco you smoke. If you are a menthol smoker, for example, try mint-flavored dark chocolate. Identify reasonable gustatory alternatives and learn to appreciate them with mindfulness to prevent mindless substitutions.

The "Mmm" Mantra

"Mmm" is a mantra of gustatory enjoyment. "Mmm" is the "om" of mindful eating. "Mmm" is the music of savoring. Practice saying "mmm" to enhance your eating enjoyment, however banal the meal. So, if you are going to eat something to distract your mouth (after you have quit smoking), then don't just eat it; "mmm" it! Practice this savoring skill now, before you quit smoking.

Renaissance of the Nose

Smoke-free life isn't just springtime for the tongue; it's also a full-fledged renaissance of the nose. Enhanced smell can be both an asset and a liability. Enjoying smells can trigger mindless overeating, but it can also, if kept in check, enhance mindful savoring and even serve as a kind of appetite-control preloading strategy. The following exercises will help you take mindful advantage of this capacity to open up your experience.

Anosmia on Demand

Loss of sense of smell (*anosmia*) can lead to a loss of taste (*aquesia*), which can lead to a loss of appetite. I am sure you've noticed that when your nose is stopped up, everything seems to be tasteless. You might have even given up on smoking when your nose was stuffed, because the cigarettes just didn't taste good anymore. As you see, this kind of temporary anosmia can be a potentially useful appetite-control tool (Somov 2008). The good news is that you can induce it on demand; you can "turn off" your sense of smell by pinching your nose with your fingers. Compare how the overall experience of different foods changes when you "turn off" the sense of smell. Try this with various foods or beverages.

You could also try throwing off your nose by applying a bit of menthol rub to its tip to block food smells. While menthol rubs are widely used over-the-counter preparations, we do encourage you to clear this experiment with your physician or dermatologist. If, in the days after you have officially quit smoking, you find that your reawakened nose keeps getting you into overeating trouble, you could also try burning some scented candles or incense.

Noseful, Not Mouthful

Preloading your newfound sense of smell after you quit smoking can help you prevent post-cessation overeating. Dr. Alan Hirsch (1998) showed that smelling food before eating facilitates fullness and reduces the amount you eat. Dr. Hirsch also concluded that the brain correlates the amount of aroma people inhale with the amount of food they take in. Apparently the more you smell the food, the less of it you'll eat. Sound too good to be true? Put your nose to the test. Active, conscious smelling of food facilitates a faster onset of fullness (ibid.). While there is still some time before you quit smoking, try this "noseful, not mouthful" approach to preload smell before loading up on food. This little mind trick will come in handy shortly.

From Fullness to "Mind-Fullness"

Smoking has been one way for you to feel full. Eating has been another. Mindfulness is the third way. The following exercise will help you practice filling up on "mind-fullness" to prevent post-cessation compensatory overeating.

Have a "Mind-full"

What's a "mind-full"? A unit of mental absorption in whatever it is that you are doing. Applied to eating, a mind-full is a moment of being conscious of eating. Make a conscious choice to notice what you are eating. Kill the TV. Put the newspaper aside. Let e-mail wait. Notice the food. Notice yourself eating it. Have a calorie of presence. You made time to be here in this moment, so be in this moment. It's just like some of your best smoking moments. They didn't all just happen on their own. Now and then, you made a point to be there, in the moment. Maybe this mindful-eating moment will last ten seconds, maybe half a minute. But whatever the length, it is a unit of awareness, a serving of mindfulness. Inhale this eating experience!

Fine-Tune Your Emotional Eating

After you quit, the continued stress of your life might be compounded by the stress of remaining abstinent from smoking, at least initially. So, you might turn to emotional eating to cope with that. That makes sense. Allow yourself that which makes sense. But to prevent emotional overeating, make your emotional eating more mindful. Remember that the problem is not emotional eating, but mindless emotional eating, which leads to overeating. Here are some exercises to get more out of emotional eating without eating more.

Relaxation as the First Course

The very idea of emotional eating is emotional self-regulation, a return to a baseline of reasonable calmness with the help of eating. To assure maximum emotional gain (rather than weight gain) from emotional eating, try a course of breath-focused relaxation before you eat to cope. This isn't a delay tactic—not at all. The idea is simple: the more relaxed you are, the less there is to cope with; the less there is to cope with, the less food you'll need to cope. Take a moment to envision this: you quit smoking, feel stressed, and want to cope orally by eating; you take a few minutes to relax, and then eat, mindfully, to cope; when you've finished, congratulate yourself on your coping success.

Low-Cal Trance

Emotional eating, as well as smoking, just like any oral coping, is a bit regressive: it takes you way, way back to those days when sucking on your thumb seemed to solve most problems. The fact is that even adults need their pacifiers from time to time. We feel that it's no coincidence that cigarettes have a much greater hold on the human mind than pipes; it's that cylindrical finger shape. The same goes for finger foods (such as chips, popcorn, nuts, candy, crackers, and so on); they make good pacifiers, because they offer that all-too-familiar, self-soothing hand-to-mouth trance. This kind of continuous nibbling is very similar to the psychology of smoking; part of the coping appeal of smoking is that it buys you time as you self-soothe with one puff after another. Pause right now to contrast and compare. Act out the smoking behavior: notice your hand go toward and away from your mouth. Now, act as if you were eating from a bag of potato chips; it's the same thing, isn't it? This is what we mean by the hand-to-mouth trance. It's a form of mindlessness on demand. Its power is in its oral simplicity.

Appreciating the relaxing power of this self-feeding trance allows you to optimize the cost-benefit ratio of emotional eating. All you have to do is keep the trance while minimizing the caloric intake. How? By substituting healthier finger foods. We suggest baby carrots and celery sticks. So, if you are stressed and feel that some snacking would help, then instead of denying yourself and risking more stress as a result, take your time to literally veg out. Have some low-calorie mindlessness on demand. Enjoy the oblivion!

Mindful Eating Isn't a Substitute for Craving Control

Let's make sure we are on the same page regarding an essential point: mindful emotional eating is not a substitute for smoking-related craving control. Say you quit yesterday, and now you have an urge to smoke; there is only one course of action, and that is for you to smoke air through this craving. Kill the craving with mindfulness-based, breath-focused craving control. Surf the urge to smoke with mindfulness-based, breath-focused craving control. Now, after you quit yesterday, if you feel stressed but don't necessarily have a craving to smoke, you have several coping options: you can use mindfulness to cope, you can mindlessly eat, you can mindfully eat, you can relax and then eat mindlessly, you can relax and then eat mindfully, or you can engage in some other, hopefully nonoral, coping behavior. So, when it comes to post–quit-date stress management, your options are plenty. When it comes down to post–quit-date smoking urges, we recommend only one option, the one you've trained hard to develop, that of mindfulness-based, breath-focused craving control (smoking air). Now we are on the same page. If not, reread the page until you feel that we are.

Conclusion: Whatever It Takes

The point of this project is for you to modify your smoking behavior—namely, to quit. If you have to gain a few pounds to stay off cigarettes, then so be it. You've got the rest of your life to address your weight concerns. Sure, obesity is a threat to your physical health, but smoking is a greater threat. So, dare to triage! Allow yourself to do whatever it takes: if you have to eat to cope, then allow yourself to eat. The good news is that you can do so mindfully, without overeating. But once again, let us be clear: eating is no substitute for smoking-related craving control. Feel free to use mindful emotional eating as a supplemental stress-management strategy, but do use mindfulness-based, breath-focused craving control to deal with smoking-related cravings. In sum, use mindful eating to keep your appetite in check and mindful emotional eating as a backup coping choice.

Part 5

The Final Approach: Testing and Quitting

So, here you are, finally—ready to take the next step. We presume you have spent your time wisely and have trained for this as if you were on fire. Our guess is that any trepidation aside, you feel both motivationally ready and skills ready. How rough of a touchdown you'll have is ultimately irrelevant. What's relevant is that you keep your wheels on the ground, one way or another. It's time to test your craving-control skillpower.

Chapter 14

Testing Your Skills Readiness

Quitting smoking is a process, not a single event.
Many users of tobacco find that they must learn to
quit before they can succeed permanently.

—Janet Brigham, *Dying to Quit*

Congratulations: you have sat on your impulse to quit smoking for some time now. We hope that you feel that you can't wait to go ahead and quit already. There isn't much longer to wait. You are gearing up for the final approach. What's left is to test your skills readiness. So, it's test week!

Testing: Craving-Control Combat—Level 3

Craving-control combat, level 3, doubles as testing. Here's what we mean: you will have the same target (the craving to smoke), the same ammo (smoking air—that is, mindfulness-based, breath-focused craving control), and the same sequence as level 2, but an even greater training challenge. Specifically, whenever you have a craving to smoke, candle-light a cigarette (without the initial drag), put it aside (to avoid burning your fingers), and start smoking air until the cigarette completely burns out. Hopefully, this sounds familiar if you completed the "Smoking Air (Riding-Free Version)" exercise in chapter 7. Now, we take it to the next level of mastery with repeated practice. Whereas in level 2, all you had to do was kill one craving, here the training goal is to kill as many recurrent cravings as it takes while waiting for the cigarette to burn out. Once you have wasted (killed) the lit cigarette with craving control, level 3, decide if you want to light another one and smoke it. Having met your level 3 objective, you are free to do whatever you want to do next. Whether or not you smoke is irrelevant; you have hit the level 3 craving-control target, so congratulate yourself on your craving-control success.

Here's the step-by-step training sequence for level 3:

1. Whenever you feel a craving to smoke, notice it and welcome the opportunity to practice craving control.

2. As you witness the craving, grab your cigarettes, go wherever you usually smoke, and sit down (if you can).

3. Light the cigarette and set it aside; open your hands, lotus style.

4. Smoke air to kill both the initial craving and any recurrent cravings, until the cigarette completely burns out.

5. After the cigarette completely burns out, you are free to light another one if the craving returns and you decide to indulge it.

6. Mentally congratulate yourself on your level 3 craving-control success.

To clarify, a successful level 3 craving-control kill means that you have endured (with the help of skillpower, not just by white-knuckling) and conquered not just one craving, but also a cigarette's duration worth of cravings. Each level 3 craving kill is one instant of passing the readiness test. Level 3 craving-control testing is as close as it gets to the most challenging craving moments ahead. For a moment, envision being on the verge of a lapse. You've been abstinent for a few weeks, something happened, and you're about to give up. You've bummed a cigarette or even bought a pack and lit up, and this is your last opportunity to take a U-turn and prevent a lapse. You watch the cigarette burn in your hands, but just because you lit up doesn't mean that you have smoked. Level 3 testing allows you to demonstrate to yourself that you can step back from even that temptation with the help of craving-control skillpower. Practice level 3 for one week, whenever you crave a smoke. Of course, the more you practice during that week, the better. At the end of the week, if you are succeeding more times than not, you've passed the test. Congratulations, you're skills ready!

Testing Is Optional

You don't have to complete the testing level. Remember, it's your life. But we suggest that you do. What if you keep "flunking" the tests? It's no big deal; the whole point of testing is to determine where you are on the learning curve. If you are not ready, simply go back to craving-control combat levels 1 and 2, and invest a bit more prep time.

Share What You Are Up To

If a trusted significant other asks you about your lighting and wasting cigarettes, feel free to let the person know what you are up to. Explain that you are not quitting yet, but are just testing your craving-control skills readiness. Clearly ask your significant others to refrain from rushing you into recovery. Realize that once others see your emerging skillpower, they might be tempted to rush you into quitting. That's understandable; they don't know your game plan and are just trying to help. Simply say, "Thank you for your enthusiasm. Right now, I am just testing, gathering some evidence; I'll let you know when I am actually planning to quit." Remember that it's okay to be tactfully assertive. Quitting at your own pace, when you feel skills ready, is the essence of this approach. Don't let others' enthusiasm and cheer derail you from your own timeline.

Conclusion: Avoid Improvisation

The point of this test week is to test your skill level. Sure, you can wing it with a random combination of avoidance, distraction, eating, and self-talk. But all of that fails to give you information about your core craving-control competence. Remember that you are building your recovery on skillpower, not willpower or chance. So, if you take the test, then test your skills.

Chapter 15

Touchdown on a
Quit Date

A one-size-fits-all approach that is too hasty...
carries a high potential for failure.

—Bess Marcus and colleagues, *How to Quit*
Smoking without Gaining Weight

Different people take different paths. Consider the ending of a relation-ship, for example. Some people take time to plan an exit, and some just up and slam the door behind them. It's the same with smoking: some quit cold turkey, and others (hopefully, you included) take time to warm up to this turkey of a project.

Soft Landing

The industry-standard quit-in-two-weeks approach to smoking cessation makes for a pretty hard landing. We hope you have heeded our advice and have been gradually reducing altitude for several weeks, if not months. Good for you! What's left is to prepare for a thoughtful, methodical final approach to ensure a lasting soft landing. It's time to check your landing gear and prepare for touchdown. And oh, yes, relax: you've done your homework, you've survived the landing simulator (by passing the skills-readiness test in chapter 14), and you've built a platform of self-acceptance and choice awareness. And chances are you can't wait to be done with this smoking-cessation project, eh? Savor the difference: in the past, when you were ready to quit, you probably braced yourself for a dreadful white-knuckle experience. This time it's different: you have skillpower on your side!

Avoid Sentimentality

A review of the stop-smoking literature reveals that more often than not, smokers are encouraged to choose sentimentally meaningful days as quit dates: anniversaries, birthdays, and so on. We guess the idea is that the smoker will be able to somehow magically convert the specialness of the day into smoking-cessation skillpower. We think this kind of approach is a sure way to ruin someone's calendar. Just imagine trying to quit smoking on your birthday. Say you lapse. How's that for a future setup for self-loathing on an otherwise special day? If you lapsed any other day, maybe it wouldn't be such a big deal. But if you lapse after giving yourself the "present" of health for your fortieth birthday, there's a good chance that it'll leave you skeptical and self-mistrustful for years. The bottom line is to avoid sentimentality; there are 365 days in a year and, thus, plenty of regular days to play with.

Take Time Off

Be pragmatic. You've spent a good bit of time and effort getting ready for this. So, take some time off and let the first day of your brief vacation be your quit date. If you have to wait a week or a month for this, then wait. Use the time in between to practice craving control. Once again, we'd rather have you feel that you can't wait to quit than dread the quit date. If time off is absolutely out of the question, then plan your quit date for the first day of the weekend. If you've got something planned for the next several weekends, then wait until you have a weekend all to yourself. Remember, timing is important.

Enlist and Educate Your Support

The fact is that if you had to quit without any social support, you absolutely could. Your smoking cessation process, as we designed it here, is built on a platform of self-sufficiency. That said, good, tactful, considerate support wouldn't hurt, of course. But that kind of support is hard to come by on its own, so you might have to cultivate it. You will need to have some role-induction talks with your significant others to educate them on what you find supportive and what you find annoying. First, take some time to ponder what worked for you support-wise before and what didn't. Ask yourself, *Do I need motivational cheerleading, or does that tend to annoy me? Do I need any additional attention, or would I prefer to be left alone?* (That, too, is a form of support if that's what feels best for you.) *Do I need anyone to prod me to use craving control, or would that just piss me off?* The bottom line is to clarify to yourself what you need and don't need, and make it known. And then clearly articulate your expectations to your significant others. Be sure to clarify that you do not expect anyone to feel responsible for your recovery success. Make it clear to others and yourself that the success of your recovery is entirely on you. Finally, recognize that recruiting meaningful support is a wonderful opportunity to cultivate emotional intimacy in your relationships. See if you can enjoy this process of fine-tuning your support system.

Avoid Declarations of Abstinence and Finality

While we encourage you to embrace this opportunity to rally your support troops, we would also like to caution you against making any demonstrative and premature declarations of lifelong abstinence. There is really no use making such definitive statements as "This time, I am definitely done for good!" Approach this phase of smoking cessation as a phase rather than a one-time event. Explain that you are prepared for the possibility of a lapse, and share your relapse-prevention philosophy. Clarify that even if you were to now and then succumb to a craving, it would not mean that you had quit the quitting process. In sum, don't rush to hang out the prematurely self-congratulatory "Mission Accomplished!" banner, but instead dig in for the long haul.

Take Smoke-Free Smoke Breaks

This is essential. First, review chapter 12, on dosed self-care, and commit to taking numerous smoke-free smoke breaks throughout the day after you have quit smoking. How often should you take a break? As often as you have a craving to smoke, or roughly as many times as you would typically smoke—at least ten to twenty times a day if you are a half-a-pack-a-day to a pack-a-day smoker. How long should these breaks be? Smoke air for approximately the amount of time it would take you to smoke a cigarette. For how long should you keep up this smoke-free smoke-break routine? At least for a couple of months; longer if it feels useful. Taking these smoke-free smoke breaks to smoke air is your best long-term insurance against a lapse or relapse. Keep the infrastructure of self-care your smoking has helped build, but ditch the tobacco. Clear enough, eh? As clear as this might be to you, the idea of taking smoke-free smoke breaks to smoke air may be confusing as hell to your significant others and even to your employer. So, you might let your employer know that you are quitting smoking, that the company will be better off for it, and that you will require brief "health breaks" throughout the day, just like your smoking counterparts. If your employer is unlikely to respond positively to such a proposition, do whatever it takes to stealthily take such breaks. You found a way to smoke while at work; now find a way to breathe (meditatively) at work. On a similar note, make sure to let your significant others know about your plan to continue to take the same amount of time for smoke-free smoke breaks. Disabuse your loved ones of any expectations that just because you are quitting smoking, you will suddenly become more available. Explain to them the importance of your continued self-care and commit to taking periodic self-care breaks, starting on your quit date, for at least a couple of months.

Keep the Platform of Breath-Focused Contemplation

This is key: this program isn't just about helping you quit smoking; it's an attempt to help you salvage your hard-earned habit of contemplative, breath-focused self-care. As you recall, smoking is a form of breath-focused meditation. We suggest that you keep cultivating this platform of contemplation throughout your life. Sure, you can use smoke-free smoke breaks to smoke air for a couple of months after you quit smoking to ensure your smoking-cessation success. But let's fast-forward to a few months after your quit date. By then you will have successfully quit, and you might question the necessity of continuing with smoke-free smoke breaks. You are right; at some point these smoke-free smoke breaks will be unnecessary as a smoking-cessation maintenance tool. But wouldn't it be wise if you continued with this habit of breath-focused, contemplative, meditative self-care for its own sake? We think it would. Let's put it this way: you, the smoker, are uniquely positioned to translate your years of smoking into years of centering contemplation. The fact is that with your habit of taking time for yourself to meditatively breathe through a paper tube ten to twenty times a day, you've logged more meditation time than most meditation teachers. So, waste not this unique habit of breath-focused presence. Keep your meditative time for yourself. Aim for a smooth and seamless transition from smoking to living a contemplative life of breath-focused presence.

Clarify Lapse and Relapse Expectations

Review chapter 11 to clarify the distinctions among a slip, a lapse, and a relapse. After that, clarify the expectations to yourself. First, the goal is not to prove anything to yourself, but to simply quit smoking. Second, it's okay to have cravings. Cravings are normal and nothing to panic about. When you catch yourself thinking that you want to smoke, that doesn't mean that you want to quit your smoking-cessation project. A desire to smoke is just a craving for you to witness and exhale. Third, it's okay to lapse. This is not permission to lapse, but simply a statement of fact: it's okay to lapse. If you lapse and smoke, that doesn't mean that you are done. If anything, it's just the beginning of craving-control combat.

Let's quantify a lapse. If you have one puff, that's a lapse; put out the cigarette and keep going as if nothing happened. If you have a whole cigarette, it's just a lapse; put it out and keep going. If you have two cigarettes back to back, it's just a lapse; finish them off and keep going. If you have a whole pack in one day, it's still just a lapse; finish it and start over the next morning. Now, if you wake up the next morning and, despite your best effort at self-acceptance, start smoking, that's no longer a lapse. It's a relapse. So, finally, if you relapse—that is, if you smoked one day and started the next day by buying a pack—it's time to return to craving-control practice until you are ready to set a new quit date.

What if you smoke less than a pack on day one and don't buy a pack the next day, but just keep lapsing with a puff, a cigarette, or a few cigarettes for the next few days? Well, you are obviously having a hard time, lapsing every so often and still climbing the learning curve of abstinence, but you haven't yet relapsed. So, in a scenario like this, keep with it until you either achieve long-term abstinence or relapse. Obviously, our cutoff for relapse is an arbitrary one: a day of lapsing with a conscious choice to buy a pack of cigs the day after. Sure, you can write your own rules on this and decide that a relapse is when you have smoked your baseline (pre–quit-date) amount of tobacco on, say, three consecutive days. But, we think you'd be missing a point. What makes a relapse a relapse is not the amount per se, but the psychology of surrender. Lapsing, if you recall, is when you fall and get back up. Relapsing is when, after the fall, you decide to stay down. So, our suggestion is that after a day of lapsing, if you wake up the next morning with the notion that you are done and are going to get some cigarettes and resume smoking as before, you don't quit the quitting process; just back up a bit and return to craving-control training until you feel ready to reset a quit date. We also suggest that you practice mindful smoking (see chapter 17) in the meantime and that you buy only one pack at a time, at a different location each time, to prevent the sense of getting back in the mindless smoking groove.

NRT: Skillpower, Not Pillpower

The smoking public seems to be under the impression that *nicotine-replacement therapy* (NRT) gizmos (patches, gums, and medications) are the standard of craving control. That isn't so! Nicotine-replacement products are designed to mediate short-term nicotine-dependence withdrawal symptoms, which have nothing to do with the long-term craving combat that befalls most smokers. The somewhat intense physical and psychological changes you experience shortly after abstaining from smoking are your body's attempt to blackmail you into compliance with its nicotine-dependent wishes. But to call these bodily demands "cravings" is a conceptual misnomer. These pseudo-cravings are just withdrawal symptoms. One way or another, with or without the assistance of nicotine-replacement gizmos, the withdrawal symptoms subside and stop being a problem. But, of course, psychological cravings remain. And no patch, gum, or pill can protect your long-term recovery from these habit traps. Therefore, the issue isn't physiological withdrawal, but *psychological withdrawal* from a long-standing habit. And a psychological issue will have to be solved psychologically. Put differently, to kill a smoking habit, you have to develop a new habit of craving control. That said, NRT is certainly a useful tool to help you take the edge off in the initial phases of nicotine withdrawal. You've been at this game of smoking cessation for some time now; chances are you've tried at least once to quit cold turkey, so you know how it is. If you feel that you can deal with your withdrawal symptoms on your own, then do; if you feel that a nicotine-replacement product would help, then consider your over-the-counter options or check in with your primary-care physician to see what the current NRT smoking-cessation aids are. Just to be clear on this, don't merely bank on NRT; there is still no magic pill to stop smoking. You'll have to use your skillpower, not just "pillpower."

Smoke-Proof Your Life (in Moderation)

The standard smoking-cessation advice is to get rid of all smoking paraphernalia (lighters, ashtrays, and so on), throw away your leftover cigarettes, vacuum and deodorize your home (wash your curtains and so on), check your clothing (for example, check your winter-coat pockets for old packs), and clean your car. This is all common sense. Certainly, do it, but in a measured way. You don't have to overdo this. The success of your recovery does not depend on stimulus avoidance, but on response control. In other words, you built this recovery effort, not on the avoidance strategy of running from people, places, and things that remind you of smoking (that's naive; smoking stimuli will catch up with you one way or another); no, you built your recovery on response control—that is, craving-control skillpower that allows you to control your response to these stimuli. So, if you invested in a pretty cool lighter and feel like keeping it, then do. If you have an heirloom ashtray, clean it up and hold on to it. Recognize that if the sight of cigarettes or some other smoking paraphernalia can easily throw off your recovery, then you are not yet ready to quit. By the same token, washing your window curtains to get the smoke out sounds like a good idea, in principle. But, in reality, it's quite a hassle, and if you are ready to proceed, there's no point in postponing your quit date over your procrastination about doing laundry. Once again, if your recovery is so frail that you can't withstand the faint smell from your smoking days (as it emanates from your window curtains or car upholstery), then you are probably not yet skills ready to quit. Make sure that you are skills ready, and you'll get to the curtains soon enough. In sum, do what you can to smoke-proof your immediate living environment, but don't obsess.

Avoid Testing

Testing is plain silly. Life is enough of a test. Worry not; there will be plenty of craving curveballs without your having to look for them. Furthermore, testing is entirely unnecessary; you already passed all the necessary tests before the quitting phase, so there's really no point whatsoever in testing yourself again. The fact is that you'll be busy enough dealing with craving control for weeks, if not months. So, put behind you this ego business of unnecessarily proving things to yourself. That's how you used to quit. This time, you need no gumption or chutzpah or ego power or willpower. Instead skillpower will do just fine. Count on *it*.

Avoid Counting Days

The original idea behind counting days is to give you a sense of confidence that you know how to stay abstinent. The problem with this kind of confidence building is that when you lapse or relapse, there is a tendency to conclude that you have lost all that time, that you are back in the beginning, in the back of the line, at day zero—which, of course, is not true. Just because you lapsed on, say, day one hundred doesn't mean that you weren't abstinent for the first ninety-nine days. Thus, counting days, unfortunately, can trigger an all-or-nothing view of the recovery process in which only consecutive abstinent days count. But that's just plain silly. All of your days count; every lived moment of this learning curve adds up to eventual freedom from smoking. With this in mind, we strongly suggest that you don't bother counting days or even weeks. Just thin the pack and remember that this time, your recovery is built on skillpower, not on actuarial self-reassurance.

Finish the Book

The next two chapters of the book (chapters 16 and 17) are about harm reduction. Read them *even* if your destination is abstinence. If you feel that reading about the harm-reduction option gives you the motivational heebie-jeebies, then that's an important clarifying opportunity. It's an opportunity to distinguish between motivational uncertainty and cravings. You see, cravings can masquerade as a crisis of motivation. Say you felt gung ho to quit smoking altogether, but after reading about harm reduction, you are suddenly not so sure. Ask yourself, *What's going on? Have my reasons to quit smoking changed, or is this just a craving?* The fact is that only you would know the answer to that question. If, at this point, you are shooting for total abstinence from tobacco, then use the next two chapters as both a final opportunity to crystallize your reasons for quitting and an additional craving-control practice opportunity. In other words, finish reading the book before you put it aside. If you are thinking to yourself, *I don't want to finish the book, because I'm afraid that reading about the harm-reduction option will change my mind*, then you should definitely read about the harm-reduction option and work your way through any cravings that threaten your motivation to quit. Face your fear, or it will face you when you least expect it. It's not as if the whole world were quitting at the same time. After you quit, you will now and then bump into those who seem to smoke in moderation, the "chippers," and you will wonder, *Maybe I could just smoke one or two like that too.* Well, we suggest you do that wondering on the front end, as part of your total, no-holds-barred preparation process. If reading about harm reduction changes your mind, then your mind wasn't certain to begin with. If reading about harm reduction bombards you with cravings but doesn't change your mind about abstinence, then enjoy additional craving-control practice opportunities—because after that (starting with chapter 18), it's quit time.

Conclusion: Just Another Day

As you read through the next three chapters, begin to schedule your quit date. But be clear on this: just because you've had to do so much planning to set it up doesn't mean that the quit date is a big deal, that it's the most important day of your life. Not at all: your quit day is just another day. There's no need for fanfare or ticker-tape parades. To think of your quit date as a very special day, let alone as the most important day of your life (as some misguided smoking-cessation programs suggest), is a setup for relapse. After all, if you, God forbid, lapse and smoke one cigarette after your quit date, instead of matter-of-factly getting back on your feet and continuing with your recovery, you'll be prone to feel that you screwed up something really huge, as if you've made the biggest mistake of your life. That's right: sentimentality, while it feels great on the front end, comes with psychologically catastrophic costs. It's true that getting to this quit point might have felt like planning a wedding, but it's no wedding. All you are really doing is optimizing your long-standing breath-focused habit of self-care by ditching tobacco. Miss the smoking bus one scheduled day—no need to chase it, wistfully watch it disappear in the distance, or madly celebrate anything—and calmly walk your way home. Just remember to review your craving-control data. If you have been collecting empty cigarette packs (as we suggested) with jotted-down craving-control kills, go ahead and gather up all the packs. Count up the dots and impress yourself with your record of craving-control practice. Allow the significance of these data to sink in. You know what you are doing. You are well armed and well prepared. You've done your homework. You have every reason to feel confident as you embark on this last leg of your smoking-cessation journey. Give yourself a pat on the back. Whatever the outcome, your effort has been spectacular! And, oh yeah, keep smoking air as often as you can.

Part 6

Destination Harm Reduction: Mindful Smoking

If all you want is to cut back, this section is for you. We didn't forget you, and we've got some stimulating new ideas for you to try. We understand that smoking still plays an important coping role in your life, that it might help you keep your cool, that it might keep you entertained in the face of existentially dangerous loneliness, that, in some form or another, it helps you live a better life. We, of course, hope that you will find other ways to cope, but throwing away a crutch before you find some other source of emotional stability is not pragmatic. So, if you flew right past part 5, past the landing strips, past the goal of abstinence, and didn't attempt the landing because you were headed toward harm reduction, you are in the right place. The following two chapters will offer you general guidelines and some exercises on how to cut back with the help of harm-reducing, mindful smoking. The last chapter will help you look ahead at the option of eventually transitioning from mindful smoking to smoking cessation, from staying cut to staying quit. As you finish the book, make a conscious choice to own your decision to just cut back. Harm reduction makes sense. It's a legitimate existential choice. Whether it's a temporary postponement of abstinence or an open-ended tour in the clouds of smoke, it is but one of the infinite ways of living life on earth. And, as far as we are concerned, if that's what you consciously choose, that's as legitimate as anything else. You aren't a kid; you know what your priorities are, so follow them without looking back, with the dignity of a self-made mind. And, should your mind change, fear no U-turns. A change of course is always a possibility.

Chapter 16

Seven-Plus Paths of Tobacco Harm Reduction

Harm reduction neither presumes nor excludes a goal of abstinence.

> —Kenneth Perkins, Cynthia Conklin, and
> Michele Levine, *Cognitive-Behavioral Therapy*
> *for Smoking Cessation*

This book has more than one audience. Sure, most of you are probably interested in abstinence, but some of you are just trying to cut back. This chapter and the following one are for you, the seeker of moderation! If you quit and relapsed (not just lapsed but fully relapsed—that is, returned to your original level of smoking), the next two chapters are also for you.

Harm Reduction: A Humane Alternative

Much of the recovery industry is addicted to black-and-white, all-or-nothing thinking. One problem with this kind of thinking is that the recovery industry sets an unnecessarily high bar for admittance to treatment. Psychologist Andrew Tatarsky (2002, 7), one of the leading harm-reduction advocates in the field of substance-use treatment, writes:

> Most treatment programs have "high-threshold" access, meaning that there are many requirements to which clients must agree to gain access to treatment: for example, urine testing, attending Alcoholics Anonymous meetings every day, breaking contact with other substance users. Clients unable to live up to these requirements are often referred for more intensive treatment, while unwilling clients are routinely discharged from treatment with the statement that they should come back when they are ready.

It's the same with the tobacco-use branch of the recovery industry: if you are not ready to quit tobacco altogether, you are deemed not ready to proceed. Nonsense! Cutting back is not a cop-out, but an existentially viable *harm-reduction* choice. But what is harm reduction? Again, Tatarsky (ibid., 2) writes:

> Harm reduction rejects the presumption that abstinence is the best or only acceptable goal for all problem drug and substance users. Harm reduction sees substance use as varying on a continuum of harmful consequences.... In doing so, harm reduction accepts small, incremental steps in the direction of reduced harm, with the goal being to facilitate the greatest reduction in harm for a given person at this point in time.

And psychologist Alan Marlatt, who was trained in the Dutch model of harm reduction, writes on the rationale behind harm reduction (1998, xv): "I began to view harm reduction as a humane and compassionate alternative to what I was familiar with back in the United States, namely, the 'war on drugs' and its punitive 'zero tolerance' approach to drug users. I began to realize that zero tolerance plus zero compassion equals zero."

Our guess is that Marlatt and Tatarsky were not necessarily thinking of smokers when they wrote about the need for the harm-reduction alternative. But they might have just as well have been. The "zero tolerance" war on smoking has been raging now for years, with smoking-abstinence zealots conducting righteous bullying psyops in restaurants, bars, and parks, as well as at bus stops and other public places. This block-by-block antismoking urban warfare has been reflected in the tobacco-use treatment industry as well: aside from being ambushed by pushy, unsolicited encouragement to quit smoking (now!) by every random primary-care provider (who doesn't know you from Adam), there are essentially no clinical harm-reduction options for smokers wishing to cut back. Don't get us wrong: as you will see in a moment, there are plenty of ideas on how to cut back and reduce harm. The problem is that the official destination point of all these cutting-back strategies is still abstinence. Harm reduction, as a means to an end, is a laudable path. We heartily recommend it. But we are not in the business of selling you our own party line: if all you want is to keep smoking but cut back, then we aren't going to close this book on you. We acknowledge a certain existential logic behind such a decision and would like to help you bring your harm-reduction vision to fruition.

Short-Term Harm Reduction vs. Long-Term Harm Reduction

Short-term harm reduction is when harm reduction is a means to eventual abstinence. For example, you decide to start cutting back until you quit. Or you tried to quit smoking, but relapsed and decided to cut back for now until you gear up for another attempt at quitting. Long-term harm reduction is when you decide that you want to keep smoking indefinitely (or until you change your mind at some indeterminate point in the future) and wish to cut back to minimize any associated harm to your health. This chapter and the next are for both audiences. So, if you prefer to go down the path of harm reduction, know this: there are at least seven harm-reduction avenues that you can take. Thus, we encourage you to shop for the harm-reduction path that suits you best. And, most immediately, you need to establish your personal risk tolerance.

What Is Your Threshold of Harm Tolerance?

As a smoker interested in just cutting back, it makes sense to ask yourself the following two questions:

- *Why am I trying to cut back?*

- *How much do I need to cut back?*

We presume that you might have one of two main reasons for wanting to cut back: health and finances. Indeed, smoking is hazardous to both your health and your wallet. With this in mind, the second question, "How much do I need to cut back?" can be restated as:

- *How many cigarettes can I financially afford to smoke per day?*

- *How many cigarettes can I afford health-wise without incurring any significant health risks?*

We aren't financial advisers, so we have no particular expertise to offer on the issue of budgeting. As for health-based concerns, we encourage you to consider the following data summary by Gio Batta Gori, from the Health Policy Center in Bethesda, Maryland, in his 2000 book *Virtually Safe Cigarettes: Reviving an Opportunity Once Tragically Rejected*:

- "[A]ll studies show a sharp drop in risk as the dose inhaled decreases" (25).

- "[P]ersons who inhale a daily equivalent to three to four cigarettes may not attain lung-cancer risks significantly different from those of nonsmokers" (25).

So, it appears that if you are looking to cut back smoking to minimize harm to your health, three to four cigarettes per day would seem to be the "virtually safe" range.

But the notion of "virtually safe" smoking isn't as clear cut as it may seem. For example, in *Cognitive-Behavioral Therapy for Smoking Cessation*, Kenneth Perkins, Cynthia Conklin, and Michele Levine (2008, 87) assert that "some of the lethal health risks of smoking, such as cardiovascular disease, are not dose dependent." On the other hand, Janet Brigham, in *Dying to Quit*, notes that according to researchers from Göteborg, Sweden, who examined the influence of smoking reduction on cardiovascular health, "...smoking fewer cigarettes per day offered health benefits for smokers" (1998, 192).

As you see, you cannot blindly rely on tobacco-use statistics. As with all matters in life, it is ultimately up to you to decide what is safe and what is not safe for you when it comes to smoking.

Set Your Comfort-Risk Threshold

Research is research; as useful as it is, it is often about no one in particular. Will three to four cigarettes be "virtually safe" for you, or not? There is no way of telling. Take a moment to ponder your general stance on life. Are you generally risk averse, a thrill-seeking risk taker, or someone in between? Ponder whether or not you are the type who listens to statistics. Take a moment to decide who you are and review how you tend to approach this sort of issue. As we see it, your personality is bound to be a factor in where you go from here. So, have an honest moment of self-assessment. Ask yourself, *Do I want to err on the side of caution, or do I want to take a chance and go against the wind of the statistics?* As a smoker interested in harm reduction, you will have to set your own risk threshold: will it be one to two cigarettes per day, three to four, half a pack, a whole pack? In sum, ask yourself, *What level of risk am I comfortable with?* And calibrate your tobacco use to your comfort level with risk. Whatever you do, approach this moment with existential courage; no one can make this decision for you. Savor this rare conscious opportunity for self-determination. Mindfully smoke on it if you have to.

Seven Paths

Just as there are many roads to Rome, there are many different paths of harm reduction. The following is a discussion of seven such paths that you can choose to take:

- Gone chipping

- Gone narrowing

- Gone fading

- Gone scheduling

- Gone high-tech (gone electronic)

- Gone low-tech (gone smokeless)

- Gone east (gone mindful)

Gone Chipping

In their book *Fast Facts: Smoking Cessation*, Robert West and Saul Shiffman (2007, 18) note that "more than 90 percent of adult smokers smoke every day" (no surprise there!), while the small remainder smokes occasionally. These "occasional smokers," also known as "social smokers" or "chippers," are "rare" and constitute "typically fewer than 5 percent of smokers." So, what exactly is chipping, and how can you get into that 5 percent of part-time smokers? Chipping is a straightforward cutting back on the amount of smoking. There doesn't seem to be any hard-and-fast way of defining what exactly constitutes chipping. It is generally defined as smoking one to three cigarettes per day, most (but not all!) days. That's right: as a chipper you may not even smoke regularly, just occasionally. Think of chipping as having a few potato or tortilla chips as you graze your way through other people's kitchens, rather than buying and eating a whole bag of chips each and every time. The fact is you probably started out as a chipper back in the beginning, when you were just experimenting; you probably didn't even buy your own cigarettes but simply bummed them off friends. Depending on what your social life is like, switching to bumming-style chipping might be a possibility. If you are around a lot of smokers and are on pretty good terms with them, then going chipping might save you not only some health but also some money. If, however, you are socially isolated or too shy to bum cigarettes each time you want to smoke, you might have to keep buying your own.

West and Shiffman (ibid.) note that while chipping seems to be increasing in popularity (both as a harm-reduction strategy and due to stricter smoking bans), most chipping rates "usually go up after a while." So, the key challenge of this kind of harm-reduction path is, of course, how to stay in your chipping range and how not to escalate your tobacco use over time. This is where craving control comes in, as well as the skill of mindful smoking, which we will cover in the next chapter.

Gone Narrowing

Whereas chipping is a straightforward cutback of the amount of smoking, narrowing is a less-direct harm-reduction strategy. The idea of narrowing is to limit the topography of your smoking life. Say you decide that you will no longer smoke at work. If you can pull it off, this choice might significantly reduce your total smoking per day, particularly if you are in a habit of doing a lot of stress-management smoking at work. The upshot of narrowing is that you don't have to worry about any daily smoking quota. Whereas with chipping, you set a goal of, say, no more than three cigarettes per day, with narrowing there is no such limit on the amount, just a limit on your smoking territory. If this harm-reduction strategy is of interest to you, the following exercise is an opportunity for you to set some situational limits around your smoking. Perkins, Conklin, and Levine (2008, 86) also wisely point out that "over time, the smoker is gaining practice being in places or situations in which he or she would normally smoke without engaging in smoking." As you see, here, too, the success of this harm-reduction strategy will largely depend on your craving-control skillpower.

Border Patrol

Start by noticing all the different smoking settings that constitute the topography of your smoking life. Do you smoke at home (outside, inside, in all rooms or just selected rooms, in bed, on the deck, on the back porch, in the garage)? Do you smoke at work? Do you smoke in your car? Do you smoke when you walk outside? Do you smoke in your friends' places? As you list these areas, determine whether any given smoking zone has traditionally been a high-smoking or low-smoking area.

Now, ask yourself how much you want to cut back. If you want to cut back a lot, make a conscious choice to no longer smoke in one or more areas where you smoke a lot. Alternatively, if you want to cut back in a stepwise manner, decide that you will no longer smoke in one or more low-smoking areas. How you go about this is your call. To help yourself facilitate these objectives, review craving-control skills (chapter 6) and remind yourself to smoke air (chapter 7) instead of tobacco in the newly established smoke-free zones of your life. To aid in this conscious border patrol, consider using a system of awareness-building reminders. For example, if you decide to no longer smoke in your car, consider sticking a plastic flower into the air vent as an alarm clock for your consciousness that this is a smoke-free area. You can, of course, eliminate the unnecessary trigger of the cigarette lighter, and you can smoke-proof your car by having it detailed. The bottom line is to redraw the map of your smoking life and use mindfulness-based craving control as your border patrol.

Gone Fading

Fading is a harm-reduction strategy that cuts back tobacco intake, not the number of cigarettes, through a stepwise schedule of switching to ever-lighter cigarettes. In *Nicotine in Psychiatry: Psychopathology and Emerging Therapeutics*, David Antonuccio and Lynn Boutilier describe "nicotine fading" as a process of brand switching, "which helps reduce nicotine dependence before the quit date" (2000, 241). In this context, we are looking at fading not as a preparatory step for abstinence, but as an open-ended harm-reduction strategy. A couple of very important points should be considered here. There appears to be evidence that when smokers switch to lighter cigarettes, they either smoke more cigarettes or inhale more deeply to get more out of less. Janet Brigham (1998, 193) notes that "recent research has shown that this particular smoking style carries the additional risk of a type of cancer seen in those who inhale very deeply, as is common in the use of low-nicotine cigarettes." So, if you decide that you'd like to follow the "nicotine fading" path of harm reduction, it is essential that you not negate the potential harm reduction of brand switching with these kinds of compensatory strategies. This is, again, where mindful smoking comes in. The idea behind mindful smoking is to help you get more out of less through the psychology of mindfulness, not through puffing mechanics. If fading is of interest to you as a harm reduction path, we refer you to *The Tobacco Dependence Treatment Handbook* (Abrams et al. 2003), which offers a nicotine fading worksheet.

Gone Scheduling

Scheduling is a way to cut back on smoking by increasing the interval between cigarettes. So, unlike chipping (which limits the number of cigarettes you smoke), narrowing (which limits where you smoke), or fading (which limits what brands you can smoke), scheduling is about playing with time. Here's how Perkins, Conklin, and Levine (2008, 84) describe this process: "[R]ather than smoking *ad libitum* (that is, whenever desired) throughout the day as the urge arises, smoking occurs on a predetermined time schedule" with the idea of "systematically reducing the amount of smoking over time by gradually lengthening the time between each cigarette." For example, you might decide that you will allow yourself only one cigarette per hour instead of random chain-smoking episodes. This can get tricky. These authors (ibid.) wisely caution that the "smoker is not allowed to 'make up' for the lost opportunity to smoke by smoking the next cigarette sooner." As you can see, the success of the scheduled harm-reduction strategy is heavily dependent on craving-control skillpower. Whereas Perkins and colleagues (ibid.) see scheduled reduction as a preparation for abstinence and encourage that "the time interval between cigarettes" should be increased "rapidly, at least every week, if not more frequently," our view of scheduled reduction at this point is strictly in the context of open-ended harm reduction. In other words, you can use the strategy of scheduled reduction as a preparation phase for chipping, and then level off at chipping. For example, you might decide that in the next month or so, you will increase the interval between cigarettes from a half hour to an hour to two hours in order to cut back from smoking a pack a day to smoking just three or four cigarettes. However you use this strategy, one thing is blatantly clear: you will need your craving-control skillpower. You will also need mindful-smoking know-how (see the next chapter) to avoid potentially unhealthy compensation through more puffing or deeper puffing, or both, and to help you get more experience out of less-frequent smoking.

Gone Electronic

In *Virtually Safe Cigarettes*, epidemiologist Gio Batta Gori writes (2000, 93): "From any pragmatic public health perspective, there could be no opposition to less-hazardous cigarettes." Chinese medicine practitioner Hon Lik must have had a similar thought when he invented the *e-cigarette* (electronic cigarette), patented in 2003. E-cigarettes come with a whole gamut of "e-juices," varying from zero-nicotine to low-nicotine concentrations to midrange and even high-nicotine doses. Refillable e-juices are sold separately and come in a variety of flavors, with some flavors designed to closely mimic popular brands. While the long-term effects of inhaling nicotine vapor are still being studied, it should be known that the American Association of Public Health Physicians (2010) has come out in support of electronic cigarettes. At a glance, it would seem that "going electronic" is a viable short-term or long-term (or both) harm-reduction strategy. Research it and try it, if you are interested. Make a conscious choice. And, just as with any other harm-reduction method, keep in mind that you could leverage additional harm-reduction benefits from e-cigarettes by plugging in your mind—that is, with the help of mindful smoking (see chapter 17).

Gone Smokeless

Going smokeless (as in switching to chewing tobacco) is certainly another harm-reduction option—that is, if you are more of a lover of nicotine than smoking per se. In *Tobacco and Smoking: Opposing Viewpoints*, Brad Rodu and William Godshall (2009) suggest exactly that: a switch to modern smokeless tobacco as a safer nicotine-delivery option. Chewing is, of course, not without its own risks and problems, such as oral cancer and gum disease. We'll leave it up to you to weigh the pros and cons of this harm-reduction option.

Gone East

"Going east" is a mindfulness-based harm-reduction approach to cutting back. While we have devoted an entire chapter to this idea (chapter 17), we feel that it is only appropriate to mention this harm-reduction strategy in this context, as you survey all of the available harm-reduction routes. Going east is not a process of subtraction: you won't have to cut back on how many cigarettes you smoke, where you smoke, or what you smoke. Going east is a process of addition: it is a harm-reduction strategy that reduces harm by adding the variable of "mind" to the smoking mix. Put simply, going east is just smoking—that is, mindful smoking. It's a strategy of getting more smoking satisfaction out of fewer cigarettes through presence of mind, not discipline.

Conclusion: Seven-Plus Roads to Harm-Reduction Rome!

In *Tobacco and Smoking*, Rodu and Godshall (2009, 55) observe that "the status quo in smoking cessation presents smokers with just two unpleasant options: quit or die." You don't have to die just yet, and you don't necessarily have to quit. The fact is that you have a total of seven different harm-reduction paths, even eight if you use any of these seven harm-reduction paths as a ramp to eventual abstinence. Whichever harm-reduction path you choose, take some time to learn about the path of mindful smoking. Adding a bit of the East to this historically Western-hemisphere habit couldn't hurt!

Chapter 17

Mindful Smoking

Thin mists and light clouds waft imperceptibly;
The friends who have gathered here pass the pipe around.
I know that there is no constancy in what is possible and what is not,
Yet I do not believe that fire and ash are only fragments of time.

—Wang Lu, an eighteenth-century Chinese
"gentleman smoker" (quoted in *Smoke: A
Global History of Smoking*)

If you decided to take the path of harm reduction, either as a short-term mindful-smoking sabbatical (as you gear up for the next attempt at quitting) or as an open-ended, long-term harm-reduction commitment, you will have to learn how to get more out of less. To do so, you'll have to shift from mindless smoking to mindful smoking. Following are a series of points to consider and a handful of suggestions to try.

Avoid Unconscious Compensation

The key challenge of cutting back is that the mind, being the trickster that it is, tries to find ways to get what it wants without consulting you. For example, if you decide to cut back, you might find yourself taking deeper puffs in an unconscious attempt to get more out of less. So, you will have to watch out for this kind of mechanical (reflexive, unconscious, mindless) compensation. Presence of mind is your best line of defense here.

When You Smoke, Smoke

Lu Yao, the eighteenth-century Chinese "arbiter of [tobacco's] taste" and author of *Yanpu* ("Smoking Manual") reminds the smoker to remember to *just* smoke (quoted in Brook 2004, 88). In particular, we learn that a mindful smoker "does not smoke when listening to the zither (the preferred instrument of [eighteenth-century Chinese] elite), when feeding cranes (symbols of longevity), when dealing with subtle and refined matters, or when looking at plum blossoms," nor should the refined and knowing smoker "be caught with a pipe in his mouth when performing a rite, appearing at an imperial audience, or sharing a bed with a beautiful woman" (ibid.). Editing out the classist sentiment, we can reduce Lu Yao's advice to the good ol' Zen notion of living in real time without multitasking. Thus, one suggestion we can glean from the tobacco manuals of eighteenth-century China is to take time to enjoy smoking.

Be Brand Disloyal

As you learn to be a mindful smoker, we suggest that you remain a free agent. Avoid brand loyalty. The reason is simple: brands *brand*—that is, enslave. Indeed, when you decide to go with a brand, you are taking the path of mindless smoking. Once you have made a choice not to choose, you are a zombie. First your tongue and then your mind go on autopilot and stop paying attention to the flavor of what you smoke. Unwittingly, you transition from a quality mind-set to a quantity mind-set, and what starts out as mindful smoking begins to regress to mindless smoking. We suggest that you never buy more than one pack of any given brand at a time, and if you can help it at all, keep experimenting with different brands. Each time you go to buy cigarettes, try something you haven't yet tried. If you have to, start ordering from online vendors and catalogs. Keep the mind-set of experimentation. Remember, novelty keeps the mind awake.

Buy Top-Shelf Brands

Mindful smoking is a pursuit of pleasure, not quantity. Let go of the money-saving mentality of buying cheap, lousy smokes. That'll cost you more money in the long term as you lose interest in the quality of smoking and revert to mindless high consumption. Remember that mindful smoking is slow smoking and, as such, is unlikely to cost you any more than the mindless, high-velocity, budget smoking you did before. So, start buying from the top shelf, and let the price awaken your mind.

Awaken the Smoking Zombie

Many of the pattern-interrupting exercises we presented in chapter 4 double as slow-smoking ways to infuse the routine of smoking with more mindfulness. We encourage you to recycle these smoking experiments as nothing less than mindful-smoking meditations. Here are a few more suggestions for you.

Try Cigar Mentality

Cigar smoking, unlike cigarette smoking, tends to be more mindful and experience driven. So, if your goal is to cut back on cigarettes, we suggest that you try thinking of them as cigars. For instance, instead of bumping one cigarette after another out of a pack, buy a pack and empty it into a humidor, and try smoking cigarettes as "singles." The idea here is to trick your mind, of course, into being more mindful. Right now a cigarette is just one of twenty in a pack that you can easily carry with you. If you dump the cigarettes into a humidor, the topography of your daily smoking will dramatically shrink. Smoking will stop being so portable and become more of a parlor pastime. Another way to import cigar mentality into your cigarette smoking is to increase the cost per unit. Stop clipping coupons and buying tax-free cartons from the reservation. Start buying top-shelf cigarettes. Now, worry not; since you are planning to cut back, your total smoking budget won't suffer. Let us clarify: cigar-ify!

Roll Your Own

Mindless smoking is largely a function of the ease of tobacco delivery. Smokers have outsourced everything but their lungs: they no longer grow their own plants, they don't cure them, they don't roll their own tobacco— heck, they don't even bother to light a match and instead rely on the thumb roll of the lighter. We recommend that you consider adding a step to this stupidly simple process: try rolling your own cigs. Experiment with loose tobacco, and either hand-roll your cigarettes or invest in a manually operated cigarette-rolling machine. The point, of course, is to take your mind off autopilot. Bumping one cigarette out of a pack is way too easy of a task to break the threshold of your mind's attention. Now, rolling your cigarettes is an entirely different matter, particularly if you roll them on a per-need basis rather than stock up. All of a sudden, a desire to smoke will involve a step of nominal, but nevertheless, labor. Wouldn't it be a hoot if, for a change, you passed on smoking because you didn't want to deal with the hassle of it? Right now, with your fully modernized smoking routine, there's no hassle, and that's a mindfulness opportunity loss!

Be Mindful, Not Lungful

On the meaning of smoking in French cinema, Dawn Marlan writes (2004, 256): "In my view, smoking in the French cultural tradition has been represented…as a pleasure that involves an experience of emptiness."

Indeed, the process of mindless smoking has a built-in vacuum of sorts, satisfying one desire only to initiate a craving for the next, or as Richard Klein writes in *Cigarettes Are Sublime* (1993, 26), "[E]ach cigarette immediately calls forth its inevitable successor." Mindless smoking is a relay race in which one and the same mind at a particular time passes on the baton of dissatisfaction to its own psychological descendent at another time.

Oscar Wilde observed, "A cigarette is the perfect type of a perfect pleasure. It is exquisite, and it leaves one unsatisfied. What more can one want?" We disagree: a cigarette smoked mindlessly does leave one empty and dissatisfied. But if smoked mindfully, a cigarette can deliver its promised pleasure. And that is exactly the point: the goal of mindful smoking (either as a harm-reduction strategy or as a stand-alone way of smoking) is to fill the mind's occasional emptiness, not with a craving for the next puff, but with a sense of self-reflective fullness. Fill your mind with smoke, not just your lungs. How? Make smoke itself an object of meditation. Instead of enslaving yourself to mindless chain-smoking, liberate yourself with a moment of pause, and allow yourself to be "thrilled by the subtle grandeur of the perspectives on mortality opened by the terrors in every puff" (Klein 1993, 2).

Savor the Smoke, Not Smoking

Mindfulness of any variety is always a mindfulness of the process, not the outcome. As you consider mindful smoking as a harm-reduction strategy, we encourage you to begin to shift your attention away from nicotine and tobacco onto the nuances and subtleties of the smoking process itself. We encourage you to become a contemplative, meditative smoker who uses smoke as a rock musician uses a fog machine, as an ambient backdrop to life's ponderings. Sure, you will have to puff to envelop yourself in this misty solitude, but we hope that at times, you will just allow yourself to let a cigarette burn like incense, entirely satisfied with it as a smoldering prop, as a meditative mandala, not unlike a lone camper squatting over the dying coals of a fire or an ancient Mayan regarding the smoking pipe as a portable altar for worshipping the cosmos (Burns 2007). Puff less, witness more; that's the essence of the mindful-smoking harm-reduction path.

Try Social Smoking

In learning the art of mindful smoking, let's take a lesson from seventeenth-century Japan. Tobacco-pipe smoking was "first introduced to Japanese high society, for example, to the samurai (warriors), the Buddhist priest classes, and some rich merchants" (Suzuki 2004, 78) many centuries ago and quickly became part of the mindful appreciation of life that consisted of "the tea and incense ceremonies, and writing or appreciating poetry" (ibid.). Of course, tobacco is no longer the status symbol that it was in seventeenth-century Japan. The fact is that tobacco has been quite a democratizer in its capacity to erase class distinctions. But that's beside the point. So, one suggestion of note from the writings of early Japanese tobacco lovers is that one way to infuse the smoking process with mindfulness is to share the experience.

Furnish the Habit with Elegance

Democratization of tobacco rid smoking of its originally cultivated elegance. Our third suggestion, based on the early enjoyment of tobacco in the Far East, is to reintroduce the element of elegance to smoking. Eighteenth-century Chinese gentleman smoker Chen Cong wrote a tobacco manual in which he emphasized the importance of proper paraphernalia (Brook 2004). The Japanese *tabako-bon* (tobacco tray), *tabako-ire* (tobacco pouch or case), *kiseru* (smoking bowl), and *kiseru-zutsu* (smoking bowl case) are examples of pre-cigarette paraphernalia in the east (Suzuki 2004). Cigarettes, of course, streamlined the process and turbocharged the smoking pace, resulting in mindless chain-smoking. Thus, the idea to consider is to reinfuse the smoking process with aesthetics. Doing so will likely slow down your smoking and help you leverage more of an experience out of each and every cigarette. How? This is where you might have to get creative. For starters, you might begin by getting yourself an aesthetic specialty lighter. Say you are smoking a pack a day and want to cut back to just a few cigarettes a day. Say you hope to limit yourself to no more than five cigarettes per day. So, put your money where your smoke is: since you plan to cut back your smoking by 75 percent, take 75 percent of your monthly smoking budget and spend it on a nice lighter. This act alone, as extravagant as it might seem, will help you slow down enough to get an aesthetic feel out of your mindful investment. Repeat the same step with next month's smoking budget and get yourself a very special ashtray. You get the point, we hope: each aesthetic accoutrement will add a touch of mindfulness to the smoking ceremony. But, of course, no object will ever replace the key ingredient of mindful smoking: mind itself.

Meditate on Miasmic Vapors

Writing about the history of tobacco, Eric Burns (2007) called this herb the "smoke of the gods." What is this enticing mystery of smoke? In their book *Smoke: A Global History of Smoking*, Sander Gilman and Zhou Xun (2004, 9 and 12) explain that right from the get-go, Europeans were mesmerized by the phenomenon of smoke:

> [S]moking, inhaling the residue of burning materials using an implement, was something that was perceived as new.... Tobacco conquered the world via the magic of smoke.... The spirit of the magic smoke has haunted human souls and bodies since the beginning of time, long before the discovery of the New World. It has to do with nostalgia for a lost world through our nose and our sense of smell—one of the most fundamental senses of our being. Smoke satisfies our craving for pleasant odors, warms our skins, comforts our souls, heals our sorrows, and brings back the sweet memories of childhood. Smoke had been always part of culture.

Smoke is a fitting metaphor for the ghostly nature of our presence, a portable 3-D hologram of impermanence, in all its ever-diffusing inevitability. We won't, of course, interpret the meaning of smoke for you. But we certainly encourage you, the mindful smoker, to meditate on these miasmic vapors. Notice what your mind projects on these Rorschach cloud patterns of your own making. Let the smoke you pass become a mirror of your own existential passage.

Enter the Cloud of Unknowing

Mists are mysterious. Be it forest fog or stage fog, cigarette smoke or the ghostly exodus from a chimney stack, clouds cloud judgment and, in so doing, reveal the illusions of knowing. Life is absurdly uncertain. At any given point in time, you are driving blindly into the unknown of what is yet to be, sometimes with nothing more concrete than the glow of the tip of a cigarette between your fingers. Dawn Marlan (2004, 261) notes:

> [S]moking is…compatible—with whatever complicated ambivalence—with existentialist absurdity.… Nihilism…best describes the link between a philosophical worldview and smoking as a way of life. In a system that calls for the reevaluation of all values,… smoking is not an activity that compromises the value of health and happiness, as much as one that argues for overcoming health and happiness as values at all.

Let's face it: there always were and, we think, there always will be people who choose their own values. The body politic of youth, in order to sell its wares, insists that mind is subservient to body and prompts people to quit doing whatever they might enjoy (be it eating fatty foods or riding motorcycles without helmets) to preserve, at all mental cost, the welfare of the body. That's certainly one path, a path of pseudo-certainty, a path that promises that a healthy body houses a healthy mind. But, of course, all too often we've seen the reverse: a healthy body with an unhealthy mind or a healthy mind in a disabled body. Just as we've been told for ages, since the days of the Roman Empire, that there are many roads to Rome, there are certainly many ways to deal with the fundamental uncertainty of existence. You can try to obsessively take care of your body, on the presumption that this will guarantee happiness, or you can enjoy yourself and pay for the pleasure of the mind with the coin of the body. It is your choice. And if you choose to smoke, own your path.

Keep Smoking Air

Mindful smoking is as much about how to smoke as it is about knowing how not to smoke when you have a craving. A mindful, harm-reducing smoker smokes just a couple of cigarettes per day and smokes air in between to deal with cravings to smoke. Therefore, mindful smoking is not just training in mindfulness, but also an ongoing opportunity for continued mindfulness-based craving-control training. As such, mindful smoking is an open-ended process of self-liberation.

Conclusion: Circle Back

As you master the skill of mindful smoking, plan to remain an amateur. We encourage you to think of yourself mindfully smoking as being on a harm-reducing smoking sabbatical. Having reached the destination of harm reduction, now and then get back in the air and return to abstinence. Metaphors aside, plan a periodic attempt at quitting, say, every six months, certainly every year, until you get it right. And remember that your mindful-smoking sabbatical is not a waste of time, but continued practice of quitting skillpower. After all, mindful smoking is mindfulness practice, and mindfulness, however you come by it, was, is, and will be an excellent platform for continued attempts to quit. So, despair not, and keep circling back from mindful smoking to mindful-smoking cessation until you finally roll this smoking rig into a hangar and hang a padlock of finality on it. In the meantime, keep smoking air and taking smoke-free smoke breaks whenever you can. Be well, fellow coper. You know how.

Chapter 18

Final Destination: Life!

The stabilization of atmospheric oxygen at about 21 percent seems to
be a mute consensus reached by the biota millions of years ago;
indeed it is a contract still respected today.... The present high, but
not too high, level of oxygen in our atmosphere gives the impression
of a conscious decision to maintain balance between danger and
opportunity, between risk and benefit. If oxygen were a few percent
higher, living organisms themselves would spontaneously combust.
As oxygen falls, a few percent aerobic organisms start to asphyxiate.
The biosphere has maintained this happy medium for hundreds of
millions of years, at least.... [J]ust how this works is still a mystery.

—Lynn Margulis and Dorion Sagan,
Microcosmos

As mysterious as smoking might be, plain old breathing is pretty miraculous in and of itself. While, on one level, this book is about smoking, it is fundamentally about breathing. Scare tactics are misguided; smoking is not a matter of life and death (dead people don't smoke, you know!), but breathing is: no breathing, no possibility of smoking. So, ignore the government's oversimplistic ways of trying to scare you into abstinence with cheesy horror shots of charred lungs and stitched-up chests. Get inspired by the mystery of breathing itself instead. Whether you are breathing straight-up, unfiltered Mother-Nature air or the flavored junk air sold by the tobacco industry, remember to enjoy this breathing journey. And be grateful for this life privilege. Thank something, thank someone, thank yourself—for being alive.

So, here you are, wherever that "here" might be. Perhaps—and we certainly hope that's the case—you have reached your final destination and quit. If so, congratulations! Or, maybe you haven't quit yet but are scheduled to quit. Then, Godspeed! Or, maybe, you are still in flight, perhaps training or testing. Take your time in practicing your skills. Or, perhaps you decided to use your newly acquired craving-control skillpower and mindfulness know-how to try out harm reduction, either as a prep phase for eventual abstinence or as an open-ended harm-reduction choice. If that's what you decided, then so be it—live your choice mindfully. There's also the chance that you have quit and already relapsed, in which case consider going on a mindful-smoking sabbatical by flying Smoking Cessation Airlines with us again. You will rule the air one day soon!

But wherever you are, we hope you can be there with a sense of acceptance of wherever you've been and of wherever you are heading. Recognize that the final destination of life is life itself.

Smoking or not, we salute your existence. We applaud your self-help effort. And, as strange as it sounds (since we don't know you), we also feel fundamentally connected to you, fellow living being, by this virtue of breathing. We—you the reader, we the authors, and all of us who respire—share one and the same existential platform of breathing.

Let smokers, ex-smokers, and nonsmokers filter their attitudes about each other through this sense of breathing commonality. Let us all be inspired by not just lungs but also each other, the ordinary ecstasy of our interdependent coexistence, and the mere breathtaking fact of being alive.

References

Abrams, D. B., R. Niaura, R. A. Brown, K. M. Emmons, M. G. Goldstein, and P. M. Monti. 2003. *The Tobacco Dependence Treatment Handbook: A Guide to Best Practices.* New York: The Guilford Press.

American Association of Public Health Physicians, Tobacco Control Task Force. 2010. "Citizen Petition to Reclassify E-Cigarettes from 'Drug-Device Combination' to 'Tobacco Product.'" February 7. Rockville, MD. http://www.regulations.gov/#!documentDetail;D=FDA-2010-P-0095-0001 (accessed May 4, 2011).

American Cancer Society. 2010. *Kicking Butts: Quit Smoking and Take Charge of Your Health.* 2nd ed. Atlanta, GA: American Cancer Society/Health Promotions.

Antonuccio, D. O., and L. R. Boutilier. 2000. "Behavioral Treatment of Cigarette Smoking and Nicotine Dependence." In *Nicotine in Psychiatry: Psychopathology and Emerging Therapeutics,* edited by M. Piasecki and P. A. Newhouse, 235–52. Washington, DC: American Psychiatric Press.

Austin, J. H. 1999. *Zen and the Brain.* Cambridge, MA: MIT Press.

Bast, J. 2008. "Smoking Should Not Be Banned in Public Places." In *Tobacco and Smoking: Opposing Viewpoints,* edited by S. C. Hunnicutt, 95–100. Farmington Hills, MI: Greenhaven Press.

Bodhipaksa. 2008. "Smoking Meditation." *Bodhi Tree Swaying: Random Thoughts of a Western Buddhist.* http://www.bodhipaksa.com/archives/smoking-meditation (accessed March 11, 2011).

Bowen, S., and A. Marlatt. 2009. "Surfing the Urge: Brief Mindfulness-Based Intervention for College Student Smokers." *Psychology of Addictive Behaviors* 23 (4):666–71.

Brigham, J. 1998. *Dying to Quit: Why We Smoke and How We Stop.* Washington, DC: Joseph Henry Press.

Brook, T. 2004. "Smoking in Imperial China." In *Smoke: A Global History of Smoking,* edited by S. Gilman and Z. Xun, 84–91. London: Reaktion Books.

Burns, E. 2007. *The Smoke of the Gods: A Social History of Tobacco.* Philadelphia, PA: Temple University Press.

Creyssel, P. 1979. "Preface." In *Electrophysiological Effects of Nicotine: Proceedings of the International Symposium on the Electrophysiological Effects of Nicotine,* edited by A. Rémond and C. Izard, 5, October 19–20, 1978, Paris, France. New York: Elsevier/North-Holland Biomedical Press.

Danysh, J. 1974. *Stop without Quitting.* San Francisco, CA: International Society for General Semantics.

Davis, J. M., M. F. Fleming, K. A. Bonus, and T. B. Baker. 2007. "A Pilot Study on Mindfulness Based Stress Reduction for Smokers." *BMC Complementary and Alternative Medicine* 7:2. doi:10.1186/1472-6882-7-2.

Eysenck, H. J., and K. O'Connor. 1979. "Smoking, Arousal, and Personality." In *Electrophysiological Effects of Nicotine: Proceedings of the International Symposium on the Electrophysiological Effects of Nicotine,* edited by A. Rémond and C. Izard, October 19–20, 1978, Paris, France. Elsevier/North-Holland Biomedical Press.

Garvey, A. J., R. E. Bliss, J. L. Hitchcock, J. W. Heinold, and B. Rosner. 1992. "Predictors of Smoking Relapse among Self-Quitters: A Report from the Normative Aging Study." *Addictive Behaviors* 17 (4):367–77.

Gilman, S. L., and Z. Xun. 2004. "Introduction." In *Smoke: A Global History of Smoking*, edited by S. L. Gilman and Z. Xun, 9–28. London: Reaktion Books.

Gori, G. B. 2000. *Virtually Safe Cigarettes: Reviving an Opportunity Once Tragically Rejected*. Washington, DC: IOS Press.

Hanson, R. 2009. *Buddha's Brain: The Practical Neuroscience of Happiness, Love, and Wisdom*. With R. Mendius. Oakland, CA: New Harbinger Publications.

Hebb, D. O. 1949. *The Organization of Behavior: A Neuropsychological Theory*. New York: Wiley and Sons.

Hirsch, A. R. 1998. *Scentsational Weight Loss*. New York: Fireside Books.

Huber, C. 1999. *The Depression Book: Depression as an Opportunity for Spiritual Growth*. Murphys, CA: Keep It Simple Books.

Hudmon, K. S., E. R. Gritz, S. Clayton, and R. Nisenbaum. 1999. "Eating Orientation, Postcessation Weight Gain, and Continued Abstinence among Female Smokers Receiving an Unsolicited Smoking Cessation Intervention." *Health Psychology* 18 (1):29–36.

Hudson Jr., D. L. 2004. *Smoking Bans*. Philadelphia, PA: Chelsea House Publishers.

Hunt, W. A., and D. A. Bespalec. 1974. "An Evaluation of Current Methods of Modifying Smoking Behavior." *Journal of Clinical Psychology* 30 (4):431–38.

Johnson, P. 2007. "One Last Cigarette Before the Firing Squad? Certainly Not!" Spectator.co.uk, August 11. http://www.spectator.co.uk/columnists/all/77801/one-last-cigarette-before-the-firing-squad-certainly-not.thtml.

Kaufman, A., and S. Gettys. 2006. *Russian for Dummies*. With N. Wieda. Hoboken, NJ: Wiley Publishing.

Kime, A. O. 2008. "The Government Should Not Tax Tobacco." In *Tobacco and Smoking: Opposing Viewpoints*, edited by S. C. Hunnicutt, 81–89. Farmington Hills, MI: Greenhaven Press.

Klein, R. 1993. *Cigarettes Are Sublime*. Durham, NC: Duke University Press.

Koop, C. E. 1998. "Foreword." In *American Lung Association: 7 Steps to a Smoke-Free Life*, by E. B. Fisher Jr. with T. L. Goldfarb, v–vi. New York: John Wiley and Sons.

Kuntz, K. M. 1997. *Smoke: Cigars, Cigarettes, Pipes, and Other Combustibles*. New York: Todtri Productions.

Lama Surya Das. 2005. *Natural Radiance: Awakening to Your Great Perfection*. Book and CD-ROM. Boulder, CO: Sounds True.

Mackay, J., M. Eriksen, and O. Shafey. 2006. *The Tobacco Atlas*. 2nd ed. Atlanta, GA: American Cancer Society.

Mandel, R. 2004. "Cigarettes in Soviet and Post-Soviet Central Asia." In *Smoke: A Global History of Smoking*, edited by S. L. Gilman and Z. Xun, 180–89. London: Reaktion Books.

Marcus, B. H., J. S. Hampl, E. B. Fisher, and the American Lung Association. 2004. *How to Quit Smoking without Gaining Weight*. New York: Pocket Books.

Margulis, L., and D. Sagan. 1997. *Microcosmos: Four Billion Years of Microbial Evolution*. Berkeley, CA: University of California Press.

Margulis, L., and D. Sagan. 2000. *What Is Life?* Berkeley, CA: University of California Press.

Marlan, D. 2004. "Emblems of Emptiness: Smoking as a Way of Life in Jean Eustache's *La maman et la putain*." In *Smoke: A Global History of Smoking*, edited by S. L. Gilman and Z. Xun, 256–64. London: Reaktion Books.

Marlatt, G. A., ed. 1998. *Harm Reduction: Pragmatic Strategies for Managing High-Risk Behaviors*. New York: The Guilford Press.

Marlatt, G. A., and J. L. Kristeller. 1999. "Mindfulness and Meditation." In *Integrating Spirituality into Treatment*, edited by W. R. Miller, 67–84. Washington, DC: American Psychological Association.

Mill, J. S. 1859. *On Liberty*. London: John W. Parker and Son.

Perkins, K. A., C. A. Conklin, and M. D. Levine. 2008. *Cognitive-Behavioral Therapy for Smoking Cessation: A Practical Guidebook to the Most Effective Treatments*. New York: Taylor and Francis Group.

Prasad, B. L. 2005. *Stop Smoking for Good: Forget the Patch, the Gum, and the Excuses with Dr. Prasad's Proven Program for Permanent Smoking Cessation*. With C. Whitney. New York: Avery.

Rodu, B., and W. T. Godshall. 2009. "Smokeless Tobacco Is Less Harmful to Human Health Than Smoking." In *Tobacco and Smoking: Opposing Viewpoints*, edited by S. C. Hunnicutt, 54–60. Farmington Hills, MI: Greenhaven Press.

Santoro, J., R. DeLetis, and A. Bergman. 2001. *Kill the Craving: How to Control the Impulse to Use Drugs and Alcohol*. Oakland, CA: New Harbinger Publications.

Schaler, J. A. 1997. "The Fifth Column: Smoking Right and Responsibility." *PsychNews International* 2 (2). http://userpage.fu-berlin.de/expert/psych-news/2_2/index.htm.

Schwartz, J. L. 1973. "Preliminary Report: Smoke Watchers Evaluation." Unpublished manuscript. Berkeley, CA: Institute for Health Research. Quoted in Smith, J. W. 1988. "Long-Term Outcome of Clients Treated in a Commercial Stop Smoking Program." *Journal of Substance Abuse Treatment* 5:33–36.

Sloan, F. A., V. K. Smith, and D. H. Taylor Jr. 2003. *The Smoking Puzzle: Information, Risk Perception, and Choice*. Cambridge, MA: Harvard University Press.

Smoke Watchers International. 1970. The Smoke Watchers' How-to-Quit Book. New York: Bernard Geis Associates.

Somov, P. G. 2008. *Eating the Moment: 141 Mindful Practices to Overcome Overeating One Meal at a Time*. Oakland, CA: New Harbinger Publications.

———. 2010a. *The Lotus Effect: Shedding Suffering and Rediscovering Your Essential Self*. Oakland, CA: New Harbinger Publications.

————. 2010b. *Present Perfect: A Mindfulness Approach to Letting Go of Perfectionism and the Need for Control.* Oakland, CA: New Harbinger Publications.

Stromberg, B. 2004a. "Static on Land: Static in Bed." *Apnea Mania.* http://apneamania.com/code/training_sel.asp?catID=1&tipID=1 (accessed May 4, 2011).

————. 2004b. "Static on Land: Walking Apnea." *Apnea Mania.* http://apneamania.com/code/training_sel.asp?catID=1&tipID=5 (accessed May 4, 2011).

Suzuki, B. T. 2004. "Tobacco Culture in Japan." In *Smoke: A Global History of Smoking*, edited by S. L. Gilman and Z. Xun, 76–83. London: Reaktion Books.

Tatarsky, A. 2002. "Introduction." In *Harm Reduction Psychotherapy: A New Treatment for Drug and Alcohol Problems*, edited by A. Tatarsky, 1–15. Northvale, NJ: Jason Aronson.

Thich Nhat Hanh. 1999. *Blooming of a Lotus: Guided Meditation for Achieving the Miracle of Mindfulness.* Translated by A. Laity. Boston, MA: Beacon Press.

Thornton, R. E. 1978. *Smoking Behaviour: Physiological and Psychological Influences.* New York: Churchill Livingstone.

West, R., and S. Shiffman. 2007. *Fast Facts: Smoking Cessation.* 2nd ed. Oxford, UK: Health Press Limited.

Pavel G. Somov, PhD, is a licensed psychologist in private practice in Pittsburgh, PA. He is author of *Eating the Moment*, *Present Perfect*, and *The Lotus Effect*. Visit his website at www.eatingthemoment.com.

Marla J. Somova, PhD, is a licensed psychologist in private practice and a faculty member in the department of psychology and counseling at Carlow University in Pittsburgh, PA. Somova received specialized training in smoking cessation treatment methods and has led multiple smoking cessation groups in hospital and community settings.

Foreword writer Andrew Tatarsky, PhD, has specialized in the field of substance use treatment for over thirty years as a psychologist, supervisor, program director, lecturer, and author. He is director of the Center for Integrative Psychotherapy for Substance Misuse, a treatment and training institute, and is author of *Harm Reduction Psychotherapy*.